Vagrancy
Some New Perspectives

This volume is published
in association with the
Institute for the Study
and Treatment of Delinquency

Vagrancy
Some New Perspectives

Edited by

TIM COOK

Family Service Units
207 Old Marylebone Road
London NW1

1979

ACADEMIC PRESS
LONDON NEW YORK SAN FRANCISCO
A Subsidiary of Harcourt Brace Jovanovich, Publishers

ACADEMIC PRESS INC. (LONDON) LTD.
24/28 Oval Road, London NW1 7DX

United States Edition published by
ACADEMIC PRESS INC.
111 Fifth Avenue, New York, New York 1003

British Library Cataloguing in Publication Data

Vagrancy.
  1. Tramps – Great Britain
  I. Cook Timothy II. Institute for the Study and Treatment of Delinquency
  364.1 48′0941   HV4545.A4   79–40623

  ISBN hardback 0–12–187550–4

  ISBN paperback 0–12–187560–1

Printed in Great Britain by
Clarke, Doble & Brendon Ltd,
Plymouth and London

Contributors

PETER ARCHARD
Department of Sociology, Polytechnic of the South Bank, Borough Road, London SE 1

NICHOLAS BEACOCK
CHAR, 27 John Adam Street, London WC 2

PETER BERESFORD
Battersea Community Action, 27 Winders Road, London SW 11

GUY BRAITHWAITE
NACRO, 169 Clapham Road, London SW 9

TIM COOK
Family Service Units, 207 Old Marylebone Road, London NW 1

JOHN LEACH
Nursing Education Research Unit, Chelsea College, University of London, Manresa Road, London SW 3

DANNY LEVINE
North Lambeth Day Centre, Royal Waterloo Hospital, London SE 1

LEONARD LEIGH
London School of Economics, Houghton Street, London WC 2

PETER PHILLIMORE
Bradford College, Great Hortom Road, Bradford, Yorkshire

Preface

The literature on vagrancy, though at first glance voluminous, is in fact quite remarkably limited in the range of perspectives it offers—far too many accounts are in the Victorian tradition of descending into an abyss. None of these has shed as much light as Turner's (1960) much more committed and undramatic study of a lodging house and its residents. The journalistic approach, as Archard (Ch. 2) and Beresford (Ch. 8) indicate, is limited at best and in danger of falsifying at worst. Equally, autobiographical accounts have rarely been sufficiently reflective to break clear of the "reformed sinner" mould. Straus (1974) has produced an almost classic biographical study of a vagrant that gained much by being pieced together over a 25-year period.

The research perspective has not sought to develop the individual case study approach, but tended rather to concentrate on the categorisation and tabulation of the vagrants and their problems. These problems have not often been viewed in a context broader than that of the individual's medical and social pathology. Vagrants have, I suggest, suffered at the hands of researchers who have shown a remarkable capacity to generalise in a highly pejorative style. Bahr (1973) pointed out that "uncontrollable alcoholism gained currency (in the 1950s) and to some extent replaced uncontrollable wanderlust and congenital laziness as the primary characteristic of the homeless man". Banks and Fairhead (1976) in a study of petty offenders in prison were ready to describe vagrants as "maladjusted" and "inadequate". It was left unclear as to whether vagrancy was synonymous with either of these concepts. It was not possible to understand how a vagrant was expected to adjust in a society where prison is a major instrument of control for offences, that may only consist of asking for the price of a cup of tea in a city street. Research from whatever discipline has to throw out more challenges and ask more subtle questions than much of it has done so far.

The perspective of the field workers has largely been confined to annual reports or project news-letters. Because most of this type of literature is written for many varied reasons, not least of which might be fund raising, insights into the nature of the problems being tackled are rare. Systematic evaluative studies of projects seeking to assist vagrants are noticeable by their absence. The account by Cook (1975) was written from the inside, and inevitably bears some of the limitations of the subjective approach.

Although some of the studies within the three perspectives mentioned above are reputable within their self-imposed limits, it is difficult to discover much valuable literature on vagrancy that strays far beyond the boundaries briefly outlined. From time to time government reports are published, but they too do not seem able to raise any fresh questions or suggest how the problems might be approached in any new ways. The Home Office Report (1976) is the latest in a long line, and in clinging to the need to punish persistent begging, for example, it does not seem significantly far ahead in its thinking of the Departmental Committee on Vagrancy of 1906.

What the present volume attempts to do is both to set down clearly and comprehensively some of the perspectives that are familiar (or we think they are), and to raise other questions through looking at the problems from a new perspective. Above all effort has been made to adopt a realistic stance, with contributions that do not avoid raising perplexing human problems caused by the interaction of the vagrant and the rest of society.

Cook and Braithwaite (Ch. 1) show that, however we may define the problem of vagrancy, to the public in daily proximity with the homeless man or woman, the issue is stark and certain: society should be rid of them. This view is a critical one for it shows the difficulties, if not impossibilities, of holding together values such as community participation on the one hand and respect for individual human beings on the other, especially when the definition of human being seems open for redefinition. The painful experience that this article represents is included because we do not wish to deny the reality of the problem that vagrancy presents for others. We cannot really remove it by, for example, an analysis based on labelling theories.

The irony is, as Levine (Ch. 5) argues, that for those individuals who themselves would no longer wish to be a problem to the general public, the way out or back (rehabilitation) is rarely looked at with realism. The very people who should be most sensitive to this issue, namely social workers, are often unwilling or unable to critically examine just what is required to help a man move from a situation where humanity is denied, to one where you are mysteriously part of normal society.

However, Leach (Ch. 4) shows, through a careful and detailed evaluative study of one large project to assist homeless men, just how severe the limits may have to be in drawing the boundaries of rehabilitation. Achieving a modicum of success, however defined in the project described, demands an enormous amount of rethinking and effort by both staff and clients. What seem to be the certainties of one day can become the questions of the next. The range and variety of services that are required, if vagrants are to be effectively assisted, shows how blinkered the past response has been: wherever there is a large number of vagrants, put a lodging house. Of recent writers perhaps only Vexliard (1957) has consistently sought to set out the subtly shifting components in the problem of vagrancy.

The punitive response that has been the dominant tone of so much of the legislation relating to vagrancy is emphasised by Leigh (Ch. 6). The sledgehammer approach of much of criminal law in this area has made it more difficult to perceive the complexity of the problems of this heterogeneous population lumped together as vagrants. In this respect the less pejorative term, homeless single person, is no more subtle in its ability to differentiate the client population.

Phillimore (Ch. 3), taking an anthropological perspective in one small-scale study, is able to show the quite considerable complexities that go into the make-up of a vagrant's life. He highlights the fine variations between groups of men that to outsiders seem indistinguishable and easily capable of being dismissed as of no serious concern or interest. More such research perspectives are needed. Archard (Ch. 2) argues that research in this field has for too long ignored the societal context in which vagrancy is deemed to be a problem. The importance of a wider view is made even clearer and given practical urgency by Beacock (Ch. 7). Campaigning on behalf of the homeless and rootless has to be part of a scenario in which, for instance, guaranteed minimum incomes are part of what society deems right and proper.

Even this book has to be seen in the light of the perspective taken by Beresford (Ch. 8) who sees much of the public presentation and discussion of vagrancy as doing scant justice to the subject matter. Trivialisation, distortion and perpetuation of myths have been the hallmark of many accounts about vagrancy. It is thus our intention to open up new debates and to offer different perspectives, not to provide easy answers, but rather to raise doubts about some of the certainties paraded as answers and truths in the past.

Tim Cook
August 1979

References

Bahr, H. M. (1973). "Skid Row." Oxford University Press, Oxford.
Banks, C. and Fairhead, S. (1976). "The Petty Short-term Prisoner." Barry Rose Ltd., Sussex.
Cook, T. (1975). "Vagrant Alcoholics." Routledge and Kegan Paul, London.
Home Office (1976). "Report of the Working Party on Vagrancy and Street Offences." HMSO, London.
Straus, R. (1974). "Escape from Custody." Harper and Row, New York.
Turner, M. L. (1960). "Forgotten Men." National Council of Social Services, London.
Vexliard, A. (1957). "Le Clochard." Dexlee de Brouvier, Paris.

Contents

A Problem for Whom?

TIM COOK and GUY BRAITHWAITE

Few organisations attempt to visit upon the middle classes the problems of rehabilitation of any so-called deviant group. As the Delancey St. Foundation in San Francisco (Hampden-Turner, 1976, pp. 62–63) put it:

> all social problems should move to where the rich people live—that way the problems can receive attention from the sector which has most control over the system that produced them . . . the reason it doesn't happen is zoning ordinances wielded by people who don't want us there. All social programmes are kept in ghettos to fester off the hopelessness . . . how do you rehabilitate a person who gets up in the morning to see everyone lined up at the Welfare Office?

Whatever the merits of trying to establish a rehabilitation facility in a middle class area the reality is that in most instances such facilities are invariably located in inner-city areas which are predominantly working class.

It is when you come to the stage of wishing to establish a facility for homeless men and women that it becomes very clear just how vagrants are perceived as a problem. It is of course true that many problem groups elicit an adverse reaction when it is your street that is to have the facility to assist the group in question. But in our experience it is vagrants who produce some of the most extreme reactions from people with little or no attempt to utter even token sympathetic noises. The theoretician tells us that "society is an active partner in producing the phenomenon called deviance and that we must look at the work of both partners if we want to understand" (Simmons, 1969). We would like to assist this process of understanding by an analysis of a public meeting in which we were directly involved. The meeting occurred because of the wish to establish a day centre for vagrants in an area of London that was marked by the number of such men that gathered on the streets during the day. Money had been obtained from both local and central

1

government to establish the centre. The building that we thought was ideal required us to obtain planning permission to change its use and this necessitated the local authority seeking the views of the residents in the area as to whether they thought the proposed change of use was acceptable. The building had been in disuse for two years and had previously been an old ambulance station.

The area in which the building was situated is a working class part of London that had already suffered considerably at the hands of the developer. Huge office blocks threaten to devour the people who live close-by. Employment is being lost. Commuters hurry through the streets to the main line station. The population is falling and schools barely seem to have enough pupils to warrant staying open. It has many of the features of all that is worst in recent inner city developments, yet for the people who still live there it is a fine community and their resilience and spirit would put many more advantaged communities to shame.

Because of the more general threat to the area already indicated, strong community groups already existed, supported in most cases by community workers. The proposal to establish a day centre for vagrants and the planning requirement to consult the local residents provided at one level a fine chance to involve large numbers in the community and make democratic participation a reality. This was so much so that at the public meeting over 150 people attended when other, and in some ways more crucial, community issues had attracted barely a third of that number. To those of us involved in wanting to set up the day centre because we honestly believed that it would be of benefit to the area by taking vagrants off the streets, it felt as if the local residents had been mobilised against us. Two members of the sponsoring committee had previously asked to speak to tenants' associations about the proposed day centre. The first and very productive meeting turned out to be the only one to which these two people were invited. Three further meetings held on the community workers' premises saw a very small attendance composed of those whose method was to take the day by force. They seemed almost to be rehearsing for the public meeting which was to come. Jacobs (1976, p. 16) states that "community action should not be used as a vehicle for one under-privileged group against another, every effort should be made to oppose any bigoted or discriminatory campaign". But in an area that sees outsiders wanting to do something for the most detested and feared group in the district it was hard for the community workers not be caught up in the excitement of an area uniting over an issue and for other views and values to remain dormant. Certainly there seemed little doubt in our mind that one group, namely the vagrants, were in a sense being scape-goated for the problems of the whole area. It was as if the impossibility of preventing other events in the area, such as the office blocks, heightened the feeling that now there was action they could take whatever anybody said.

Sills (1976) has outlined clearly the reactions of a local authority itself to the efforts to establish and run a night shelter for homeless men. Some of the issues raised and attitudes adopted were paralleled at the public meeting which we now wish to describe. Beresford (1977) has also briefly described a meeting uncannily similar in feeling and content to the one analysed here. What we wish to stress is how the local people saw the problem, for in fact the local authority councillors were mainly in favour of the project and had over many years been supportive of many schemes to help the vagrant population in and around their particular Borough.

Within two or three minutes of the meeting starting the Chairman had twice stated that we were dealing with an "emotive item" though the packed hall would have left no stranger in any doubt at all. The subject matter was clear if hard to define: "we don't have to ask ourselves what it is about . . . it is about the people you would see hanging around in our neighbourhood". It was stated that the proposed day centre was "to help these people but also to help us".

The main address from the proposer of the day centre failed to go beyond five minutes before the Chairman said "we seem to have broken down basically" and had to curtail the remarks of the day centre proposers. This arose simply because the fearful and blind zest of the hostility against the day centre was stronger than any force on the other side. The first speaker had sought to be reasonable and fair in an attitude that bore no relation to what the residents were desperate to say. Assurances that we "really wanted to listen to other points of view" and that we wanted "to conduct the evening in a spirit of fairness and had no intention to pull the wool over anybody's eyes", had no relevance. A rational attempt to explain why money was being spent on a day centre for vagrants in an area that was short of play space for children was thought to be necessary by the proposers of the scheme but made little sense to the audience—even supposing it was actually heard. It was in fact a scheme founded by the government within money earmarked for such schemes and not available for any other community resource. Portraying the vagrants as human rather than "grotesque creatures", who though homeless have lived in and around the same lodging houses for many years, was again irrelevant and totally unsatisfactory as offering even the remotest justification for proposing a day centre in the neighbourhood. The explosion occurred when the speaker said that it would be fine to have the centre in a more prosperous part of London but the vagrants would never go, "the residents wouldn't have them", roared a member of the audience. "We don't want them here" shouted another. From then on the meeting was more and more difficult to control.

A local middle-aged female shopkeeper came to the front and echoed fairly accurately how people saw the issues:

I have been beaten up a number of times by these people. I was beaten up on Tuesday. I have lived and worked here for 12 years. I work in my shop 12 hours a day and there are people here who want to put a centre for these men next door to me. They come into my shop when their social security money has gone and they beg food from me. They accost young people in the streets. They strip in front of me, they have sex on the green, they couldn't care less where they have sex. That's the kind of people you want to put next to me.

Anger at the proposers of the centre was joined with cynicism about the council: "if we don't have this meeting tonight then they are just going to go straight ahead with it and we are going to be stumped". This was followed by long applause.

By now the Chairman was ready to say that:

it seems to me quite clear that the proposed site is out as far as the day centre is concerned. Now I think that the question is whether we can leave it there or try to face up to the problem of what do we do in the neighbourhood in general?

This question, however, remained unanswered for a key local spokesman made a major attack on the proposers:

One thing that has become more and more evident during the past few weeks is that the instigators of this diabolical scheme do not live in the area . . . when their day is over the nightmare will begin for the residents. Have their wives, sisters or mothers ever had to witness the disgusting acts which are daily occurrences in the local park? No, of course not, they don't have this kind of thing where they live.

The local councillor was also rounded on for "of course where he lives they don't have this problem".

The question then arose of the numbers who might use the centre or be attracted to it:

There is an outside chance of 1250 men using the proposed centre. This we find totally unacceptable and believe that before any provision is made for spending £68,000 on outsiders the council should ensure that we are providing chemists shops and other facilities sadly needed. How anyone imagines that they are assisting the community by proposing such an undesirable venture is beyond understanding. If they were under the impression that we wanted something done about vagrants they certainly misunderstood exactly what we wanted done (applause). To further prejudice the safety and happiness of the majority of the residents of the area for a minority who do not even originate from London does not make sense.

Shortly after this a former vagrant spoke urging the community to "help other men" like himself. He was brave enough to say "you are not going to help yourselves by persistently sending the problem somewhere else". Uproar broke out and shouts of "go back to where you were born" were prominent. The intervention of a self-confessed vagrant, former or not, provoked a stream of comments about the behaviour of vagrants: "they utilise all the seats in the park", "no residents sit on those seats otherwise they'd catch vermin", "all they do is drink methylated spirits and smoke and get food from the church", "they urinate against the fence and I've seen a woman kneel down and wash her hands in it", "if the police do put them in a van they've got to fumigate themselves and their own uniforms", "they expose themselves to the children as they come to and from school", "they can't get anywhere to sleep for they won't have them", "the bus garage has been wrecked five times this year", "the police won't touch them because if they take them to court they give them a meal, a good night's sleep and then they go on their way".

At this stage there was an attempt to intervene by the worker at a day centre for vagrants in an adjoining borough. He began to explain how ten years previously his centre had opened under local protests but was now welcomed because it did in fact keep many men off the streets during the day. The intervention of "where do you live?" again occurred and the explanation that he lived round the corner from the day centre was responded to by "I don't care where you live, I live here". Whilst the Chairman thought the speaker had "thrown a little light on the other side", it was hard to see how in the mood that was now so clearly established.

The attack again shifted to the councillors who were present and who were invited to speak. The Chairman of the Social Services Committee tried to place the day centre in the wider context of the whole social services budget:

> In Social Services we spend nearly £12 million a year. Nothing has been spent on dossers. The money is spent on things like child minding, fostering, day nurseries, play groups, old people's homes, care for the physically handicapped and mentally handicapped, lunch centres . . . all these are for people who are in need and who want help. The people I haven't said anything about and who you have been talking about are the dossers, who have nowhere. Now these people were once human beings like you, were husbands and unlike us through some misfortune or other they are now not working and they hang about.

The effort to give the issue a context now provoked a counter-attack, similar to one made earlier in that the Councillor was derided for not living in the area. The reference to work was also a signal for shouts and comments about the "scroungers". The style of the Councillor was criticised by one vocal resident as being one of "let's humour them" and anger expressed at the apparent suggestion that "we are no better than any of them . . . this isn't true, this isn't true, this isn't true". The Councillor did plead with the residents "just to think that if you do say that you don't want anything to do with them you are, in a sense, just living with what you've got". But as one of the residents replied, "I say that we don't want it and it's as simple as that. We do not want them in this area whatsoever".

The Chairman then put the question of whether the residents wanted any sort of scheme in the area, agreeing that the original proposal was "already written off, long ago, more than an hour ago". But the issue was then raised of whether the Council was actually going to take any notice of what had been said. Another Councillor came forward to try to suggest that there were ways of getting the vagrants off the street and that he had lived happily near to an alcoholics recovery centre for some years which had shown just how with the right kind of measures rehabilitation was possible. The area had to face the fact that short of physical deportation the Councillors could not clear the streets for "we cannot move the bulldozer in and move them away". The possibility of an alternative site again produced the response directed very much against the outsiders, in this case the local authority. "If you want another site, there's room, right next to County Hall, you might want to take some notice of them then. There's the little back roads there, we'll stick them in there and we can't see them and they will no longer be our responsibility". The Councillor however returned to the problem that vagrants had been in the area for "donkey's years . . . these people are there and we have to find someone to deal with the problem. This problem exists and we have to find a solution for it."

This insistence that some solution really ought to be found, led to a feeling that further reassurances were needed from the Councillors. As one resident put it "if we say no, can you promise us the day centre will not go through?" A few shouted that the "decisions have already been made" to which the Councillor replied "I give you my complete assurance it has not been made. What I also say is that it's very clear from this meeting that there is no community support for this proposal. I doubt very much whether the scheme will be approved." But still a man shouted "what you are saying is that it has already been agreed!"

A final effort was made to point out to the residents that eventually some effort would have to be made to tackle the problem. "Nobody can go back to transporting people away." "Why not?" came the reply. "Surely you're not suggesting we hang them." "Yes, hang them," came a number of shouts. Eventually amidst a growing babble the Chairman was able to put to the meeting whether they would wish to have any project for vagrants in the neighbourhood. By 135 votes to seven the community clearly expressed the view that no day centre of any description would be welcome in the district. The Chairman concluded:

> I would like to say in closing this meeting that I think we have survived a rather hectic meeting and I hope that those of you who don't usually come to these meetings will come to other meetings when there are other subjects for discussion, matters of similar importance in the neighbourhood.

To our knowledge there has not since been a matter of similar importance, at least if the numbers attending are an indication of that importance. The questions, however, remain as to why the homeless vagrants are seen as such a problem and why the reactions are so fearsome.

At root the vagrants do seem to represent a set of values at variance with, or deviating from, wider societal values. Essentially the single homeless are seen as "undeserving" because of the values ascribed to them. Cooper (1976, p. 56) has summarised these:

> they work infrequently if at all, and are irregular and unpunctual in dealings with agencies; they are frequently dirty and unkempt in appearance; they have an irrational, chance-centred approach to life that precludes rational planning and problem solving; they are thought to be unpredictable and uncooperative. Certainly this is often how vagrants are seen and some may be accurate statements of the situation seen from the outside. The problem is that these are not necessarily values but consequence of the inadequate services provided in the first instance for those who have become homeless. For example the conditions in many lodging houses mean that individual lockers in the bedrooms cannot be provided for personal belongings and theft from the mass lockers in hallways is not uncommon. This can too often mean that individuals soon develop a casual attitude to property, an attitude learned from their guardians which then becomes ascribed exclusively to the homeless.

Whatever values we ascribe to the homeless they still seem to be defined as deviant rather than say eccentric. What becomes crucial is "the societal values the single homeless appear not to share" (Cooper, 1976). In an analysis of the last century's approach to deviance Pearson (1975, p. 163) has shown with remarkable insight how "sewage and drains were guiding metaphors for those who depicted the deviants of this time". This then reappears in muted tones with the homeless in the late twentieth century. They now are increasingly seen as residue, the waste that is left over from the normal processes of society. As Cooper (1976) states: "they are in fact waste (in the socio-economic machine)—whether they are to be seen as a waste product or unusable in the first place is irrelevant; the point is that they form a human residue".

As a wasted or wasteful group they attract such an inferior status that they may in the telling phrase "experience conceptual liquidation" (Pinker, 1971, p. 140). But as we noted in the meeting described above others can go further and call for their actual liquidation.

The sorts of phrases that are used at public meetings clearly show how this group offends the dominant values; they do not work, they lie around, they get money for nothing, they abuse us and dare to beg from us who have worked hard for what we earn. In other words the vagrants seem to offend or even challenge the values that seem vital for the sustaining of the industrial society in which we live. Even worse they even at times seem to enjoy the deviant state—this is only a superficial observation many make of a complex scene, but it is nonetheless an observation which can all too easily shape attitudes.

Coupled with the fundamental clash of values that vagrants seem to engender is an equally powerful element, namely that of an outside group
actually taking over the stable society of the insiders, the majority. "Invasion"
is a word that occurs repeatedly in most journalistic accounts of any local
anxiety about homeless people. Vagrants are said to "lurk" in subways, almost
suggesting an urban guerilla force. In other words it is not just that vagrants
seem to defy the values of the industrial society, they are actually threatening
to disrupt our own order of things. They are invaders. This has deep roots.
Rothman (1971, p. 19) examined in his history of the asylum, early American
colonial attitudes to outsiders and wrote: "the poor stranger, the vagrant or
the wanderer, without these credentials (good standing and occupational
skills) was to be excluded. He might become not only an expense to the town
but a cause of disorder". Savage punishments were not directed at poor locals
but at outsiders. In nineteenth-century London Stedman-Jones (1971, p. 286)
has suggested how there was anxiety in the city because of the massive influx
from the countryside which might actually bring about a "progressive
deterioration of the race"—almost a genetic invasion. With the asylum no
longer a major means of maintaining social order, the free vagrants on the
streets can evoke the most fearsome reactions as people's values and very
settlement seem under attack.

In this context the sexual fears become clearer as the alleged flagrant sexual
and bodily misconduct of the vagrants reaches the most private areas of
people's lives. The invading army not only pillages but rapes. The intensity
and frequency with which allegations of sexual misconduct are made against
vagrants is always alarming and invariably at considerable variance from the
knowledge and experience of workers in the field. Nonetheless the fears exist
and cannot be lightly dismissed. The disorder that the outsiders can cause is a
very real threat. Rolph (1970) quotes a resident at a meeting to discuss a
hostel for homeless ex-prisoners as saying they will be "a menace to the area".

The fears are in a sense compounded by that fact that very rarely is anyone
within the community advocating some form of assistance for the vagrants.
It is another group of outsiders who are urging that something positive is
done for the group that seems to threaten what all the community stands for.
Again the regularity and style with which the outsiders, the professionals,
are challenged is striking. Sills (1976) quotes a Councillor, this time attacking
the do-gooders very much as we were attacked in the meeting already
described:

> I am not interested in the do-gooders who have been writing to the papers to
> say what a great service this (a shelter for homeless men) is to the community.
> They do their stint, salve their conscience and go home. People who live there
> have to live with it all the time, and I think they are entitled to have their say.

Beresford (1977) writes of people bawling "where do you live?" at someone
in favour of a centre for vagrants.

While Kosviner (1972) has related how it is possible to overcome initial local opposition for the establishment of an unpopular facility—in this instance a hostel for ex-addicts in a middle class area—the fact remains that many community problems are concentrated in the same areas of the community. It is not the affluent and well-organised sections of the community that are threatened by vagrants, either as individuals or in a facility, but rather the areas that are already under stress. There may be a sense in which because the vagrants are so personal in their contacts—they beg—and so visible—they sleep on park benches—it is easier to marshal one's forces against them. When in the same area housing sites are lost to developers for huge office blocks it is extremely hard to know whom to fight, when and how. It is ironic that some vagrants are as appalled by the value systems of planners and property developers that destroy communities as are the residents in inner city areas that seek to drive out the vagrants. They do have much more in common with the pervading value system than we realise or are prepared to admit. Church (1964) for example wrote of the tramp poet, W. H. Davies, that: "his genius gave that life (of vagrancy) a Stevensonain glamour—but I observed that when he began to earn a little money from his writings . . . he gave up sleeping in doss-houses and settled in a cottage in the village of Weald". There is every evidence to suggest that many homeless men and women today would do the same whether earning money from writing or in rather more prosaic ways. It is, however, extremely difficult to obtain a foothold in the wider society when you are seen as part of a group so deviant that hanging is urged as a solution.

Beresford (1977) quotes the official supporting a residential centre for vagrants saying at a public meeting to over 200 local residents "I know your fears are real but you'll find they are not supported". Some people do know that vagrants do not rape and pillage, but there is still a gap in our understanding of why vagrants are seen as such a threatening problem. It is not a debate in which appeals to sense have a part to play, yet it is not a debate we can leave to the academics. Gill (1977, p. 2) puts this point rather well: "mention the term social problem and the academics' immediate rejoinder is to ask who says it is a problem and who is it a problem to. My answer to these questions is unequivocal—the creation of the delinquent area is a social problem to the people who are forced to live there". Local communities then will always win against proposals discussed in this chapter. They are stronger in number and passion. If you think there are plans to store refuse in an expensive box in your street you scream, and the powers that be are frightened by the din.

References

Beresford, P. (1977). Hostile reception. *New Soc.* **41** (78), 600–601.

Church, R. (1955). "Over the Bridge." Heinemann, London.

Cooper, P. (1976). "Problems of Provision for the 'Undeserving' Homeless." M.A. Dissertation, Manchester.

Gill, O. (1977). "Luke Street." Macmillan, London.

Hampden-Turner, C. (1976). "Sane Asylum." San Francisco Book Co., California.

Jacobs, S. (1976). "The Right to a Decent House." Routledge and Kegan Paul, London.

Kosviner, A. (1972). "Unwanted Neighbours." Mental Handicap Conference, London.

Pearson, G. (1975). "The Deviant Imagination." Macmillan, London.

Pinker, R. (1971). "Social Theory and Social Policy." Heinemann, London.

Rolph, C. H. (1971). "Homeless from Prison." Report of the Special After-Care Trust, London.

Rothman, D. (1971). "The Discovery of the Asylum." Little, Brown, Boston.

Sills, P. (1976). Voluntary initiative and statutory reaction: a study in the political control of social reform. *Comm. Dev. J.* **11** (2), 120–125.

Simmons, J. L. (1969). "Deviants." Glendessary Press, USA.

Stedman-Jones, G. (1971). "Outcast London." Oxford University Press, Oxford.

Vagrancy—A Literature Review

PETER ARCHARD

Introduction

The central purpose of this paper is to review some of the more important literature on vagrancy in Britain. Of course, it would be impossible, even if desirable, to offer a comprehensive review of the literature. This review is necessarily selective, both in terms of the substantive issues I wish to stress and the theoretical and methodological perspectives which have guided researchers in their investigations.

The review focuses on that work broadly sociological in its intent and content, that is studies informed by a method of enquiry and a theoretical perspective claiming to be scientific. Immediately an important problem is posed. Limiting the review to sociological studies means that certain types of work, some of them significant in their own right and containing valuable sociological insights, will be ignored. Three types of work on vagrancy are thus excluded from this essay. First, there is a well-established tradition of literary and journalistic work on vagrancy based on the personal observations of its authors not touched upon here (Davies, 1971; Sandford, 1971; O'Connor, 1963; Orwell, 1949). Second, I have chosen to ignore that body of work stressing the purely medical and pathological aspects of vagrancy (Laidlaw, 1966; Edwards *et. al.*, 1966; Crossley and Denmark, 1969), except where they are explicitly concerned with the social consequences of disease and mental illness and thus offer social policy prescriptions by way of tackling the problem. Finally I have chosen to leave out that literature, particularly prevalent during the last century and first half of the twentieth century, underscoring the moral and spiritual dimensions of vagrancy and destitution (Booth, 1890; Smart, 1935). This last body of work, inspired by the religious zeal of its

11

authors, offers mostly anecdotal accounts of destitution amongst Britain's more visible underclass, often with an eye to their moral and spiritual salvation.

Even then, the specifically sociological literature is considerable in quantity, scope and quality, if only because investigators focusing on the social aspects of the problem have drawn on a number of quite distinctive theoretical and methodological frameworks to understand and explain the same social phenomenon. Accordingly, the implications for social policy and direct intervention in the problem vary too, flowing as they do from the different explanatory frameworks used.

There is a second purpose to this chapter. By way of complementing the literature review I attempt to spell out a framework indicating in what directions fuller and more systematic investigations into vagrancy may be most fruitfully pursued. I argue the necessity for going beyond the present levels of theorising and practice in relation to vagrancy, mainly because I believe that our current understanding and practice is essentially lopsided and partial.

There are two potentially positive spin-offs in outlining a new framework for the study of vagrancy. Firstly, the perspective will serve to identify both the shortcomings and advantages of the literature reviewed. Secondly, shifting the initiative to the reader, hopefully the other essays in this collection will be critically judged against the new framework. In such a way I hope the debate about the nature of vagrancy in contemporary Britain, both at a theoretical and practical level, will be taken forward.

Towards a Fully Social Theory of Vagrancy

I wish to start by developing a theoretical position. The reason for using theory as a point of departure is the necessity to grasp from the outset the central features of vagrancy which writers have chosen to stress. This will enable us to appreciate that, so far, we have not had the advantage of a comprehensive account of the problem.

What is meant by a fully social theory of vagrancy? In a nutshell, the problem requires an integrated theoretical and practical grasp which takes us beyond focusing on selected social aspects of the problem in isolation of a radical understanding of the political–economic, cultural and structural forces which have shaped, and continue to determine the shape, of the problem. Furthermore, such an understanding needs to be historically informed.

Vagrancy is essentially a social problem, no more and no less. This assertion may appear on the face of it to be obvious. A careful unpacking of the meaning behind it, over and against the emphases contained in the literature reviewed below, will hopefully reveal otherwise. Suffice it to say that, without exception, investigations into vagrancy have been only partial and, more important, conservative or liberal in their implications for the formulation and intervention of policy. The predominant thrust of virtually all the literature on vagrancy separates the problem, and policy directed at it, from the wider society in which it is located. It denies the historical specificity of the problem, particularly the way in which the extent and form of vagrancy varies during different historical stages in the development of society. In addition most analyses avoid making any connections with the unequal distribution of political, economic and social power in our society as a relevant backcloth to understanding the issue and thereby acting towards it. From a structural point of view the concepts of class and class consciousness are insufficiently grasped and used in a sociologically critical sense.

The most important assumption underscoring contemporary sociological analyses of social problems—including our understanding of vagrancy—is the reformist stance adopted towards the consequences of social problems (Cohen, 1974). Without exception, the root causes of social problems, problems of economic poverty and exploitation are ignored. Instead a reformist stance remains locked within the narrow confines of reducing policy and practice to the results—not the causes—of pathology and inadequacy. It stresses the individual emmiseration of this or that vagrant, and promotes a social practice to save, correct, treat or rehabilitate him by the establishment of social control institutions reflecting such an individualistic approach.

In this light social problems are viewed as peripheral blemishes in an otherwise equitable and open social system. Insofar as social problems are acknowledged as in need of correction and amelioration—or indeed even abolition—then what is seen as necessary and appropriate is piecemeal reform of one kind or another. To regard social problems—particularly those which have their roots in institutionalised poverty and exploitation—as an integral and endemic part of a capitalist social structure, would be to call into question that very structure itself. Even a casual acquaintance with the development of mainstream contemporary sociology reveals that this critical questioning does not inform our explanation of social issues. Deviants, criminals, outsiders in general, and sectors of the community who fall prey to poverty and destitution, whether through economic forces or institutions of social control impinging on their lives, are only viewed as legitimate targets of intervention inasmuch as they may be reintegrated into the wider society. That society itself rarely comes in for radical analysis for producing the problem in the first place.

In short, those institutions vested with power in our society—government departments, at local and national level (policy makers, civil servants and politicians), and the institutions at the front line of social control (prisons, courts, the police, mental hospitals, etc.) are not informed in their practices by a radical theory of social problems. They are merely engaged in a mopping-up operation. It is my view that in order to alter both the consciousness and practice of those involved in social problems—whether they be the victims of an inequitable social system or those persons engaged in reforming that system—a much more comprehensive and radical theory and practice is required. This achievement will not come overnight. Neither will it be easy.

When we look at the literature on vagrancy it soon becomes apparent to what extent this critical focus is absent. Rarely, if ever, is vagrancy in its contemporary form, understood as basically rooted in economic factors flowing from the class nature of our society. Poverty, homelessness, chronic unemployment, institutionalisation and personal demoralisation—features that characterise vagrancy and emanate from economic inequality, are responded to by avoiding structural factors and stressing the biographical details of vagrants' moral career. Thus we have a large corpus of empirical investigation and social practice underlining the individual pathology, immorality and inadequacy of vagrants and thereby promoting their reform, care and rehabilitation as individuals. The institution of vagrancy, as one concrete expression of class divisions within our society, is avoided.

That this is the dominant, indeed almost exclusive, characterisation of vagrancy, and attempts to control it can be demonstrated by asking how often are some of the following questions systematically pursued by contemporary investigators. Why does vagrancy continue to exist in a stage of advanced capitalist development when that development, in terms of social policy and a universal welfare state, is said to have resolved the iniquities of a *laissez-faire*, entrepreneurial and highly competitive economic system? How is it that we ignore such crucial structural factors as the occupational, ethnic and class origins of vagrancy in terms of the dynamic relationship between classes historically informed? Why do we choose to ignore the fact that so many of the features and institutions of vagrancy—begging, petty crime, sleeping rough, casual work, common-lodging houses, reception centres (a direct descendant of the Poor Law workhouses), soup kitchens and shelters, imprisonment and the mental asylum—indeed, the very life-style of vagrancy and methods of controlling it, continue to exist well into the twentieth century, very much in the way of previous centuries? Why do we fail to take into account economic booms and slumps, depressed economic regions, poor housing, schooling, health facilities, occupational opportunities and working conditions as central generating forces in the continued reproduction of vagrancy and its attendant ills?

Because our energy is directed at resolving the personal manifestations of vagrancy, manifestations which are articulated in terms conceptualising vagrants as socially inadequate, anti-social, immoral, spiritually weak, feckless, pathologically diseased, mentally ill, and so on, the types of questions posed above are bypassed. This is not to argue that we should ignore the biographical dimensions of vagrancy. Indeed, any attempt to work with vagrants for their improved welfare and health must take into account these important aspects of the problem. But we must comprehend these dimensions within a theoretical and practical framework which allows for the inclusion of structural and institutional components such that our vision of the problem is extended to a radically political appreciation of the task involved in the long-term abolition of the conditions which give rise to the problem in the first place (Cohen, 1975). It is all too easy to explain away social problems in our society as somewhat incidental, when the dominant belief is that we have achieved a social system where standards of living, health, education and work are such that the class nature of capitalism is regarded as a bygone of the early stages of industrial development. But the very rhetoric employed by those persons manning the master and middle range institutions of social control—civil servants and politicians in the central and local government bureaucracies, and social workers, psychiatrists, law enforcement officers and other caretakers of the dispossessed working in front-line agencies and institutions—conceals the deep rooted inequalities of wealth and power which generate and sustain the problem.

Vagrancy is only one manifestation of the most acute and visible form of class poverty and powerlessness. In vagrancy we have, concretely expressed and in its most concentrated form, the entire range of problems which at some time or another, and in part directly, affect large sections of the working class in contemporary Britain: homelessness, poverty, unemployment or under-employment, institutionalisation, ill-health and social disaffiliation.

What is required to tackle these problems, it is claimed, is the introduction and implementation of reformist strategies seeking to rescue individuals from this state of affairs by methods of individual rehabilitation and care, as if the only problem is the reintegration of those individuals affected into the mainstream of capitalism. I am here offering a critique of two interrelated levels of reformism: (i) the administratively-based policy work of politicians and civil servants who are one step removed from confronting the problem directly; and (ii) the correctional and rehabilitative strategies and techniques of front-line agents such as psychiatrists, social workers of one form or another, and the personnel manning police stations, courts and prisons. The significance of the above critique also lies in two directions. Firstly, it is of paramount importance that theorising about vagrancy makes a break with the dominant thrust of contemporary explanations about the cause and nature of the problem. Secondly, any practical spin-off from such radical theorising has to demonstrate that, in tackling vagrancy, there is a need to move beyond the strategies and tactics of reformist front-line practice. The way in which the sociological literature on vagrancy has avoided or confronted a radical theory and practice will now be examined.

A Selected Literature Review

What then, theoretically and substantively, has some of the major sociological literature had to say about the nature of vagrancy and society's reaction to it? In particular I want to draw out the advantages and shortcomings of the literature against the outline of radical theory spelled out above. For the most part, as I will go on to demonstrate, the dimensions of a radical theory have not been invoked by social investigators in explaining the phenomenon.

No analyses of social problems are possible without a specific framework or perspective, however implicit, informing our intellectual and practical grasp of the problem. Systematic investigation of social problems reflect the theoretical and methodological developments in specific social science disciplines, or the ideological and moral predispositions and values of individuals writing about social issues. Thus history, law, psychology, psychiatry and sociology have offered different accounts of vagrancy and solutions to it.

This is not the place to outline the distinctive development of theoretical frameworks and perspectives used in analysing social problems. To do so would take us into the realms of the philosophy of science and ideology, a task well beyond the scope of this paper. Only insofar as the literature on vagrancy is being reviewed will I touch upon the theoretical, methodological and substantive concerns of specific works. A critique of the literature in terms of these issues will enable me to establish a point of departure for taking our understanding of vagrancy forward.

Historical Accounts of Vagrants and Vagrancy

To this day a comprehensive sociological history of vagrancy in Britain has not been produced. Certainly no structural analysis, using a radically informed perspective in which the economic and social conflicts of opposing classes is invoked as a guiding framework, has yet been written. Such a perspective would need to scientifically demonstrate, using the method of dialectical materialism, whether vagrancy in its distinct forms, was the product, in the final analysis, of socio-economic forces.

At best, our historical grasp of vagrancy in Britain is derived from writers investigating the relationship between economic conditions and specific legislation aimed at curtailing or controlling vagrancy (Chambliss, 1964). The shifting concerns of legislators in meeting the problem under changing social and economic conditions has been revealed through bringing together a sociological analysis of law in the context of economic history. Unfortunately no comprehensive study of this kind has been attempted. All we have is a limited number of partial histories, some more sociologically informed than others, but all lacking an awareness of the relationship between social structure and economic forces. Prior to the mid-nineteenth century our primary sources of data are exclusively documentary evidence focusing on the promotion and implementation of legislation. Thus a history of vagrancy can be constructed, but it is a history from above, that is a history viewed from the position of power held by legislators with a vested interest in controlling the problem (Pound, 1971). Only in late Victorian Britain, through the work of Booth (1901) and Rowntree (1901) do we begin to receive a hint of an insight into the psychology and culture of vagrancy in a specific historical period, since their main concern was with the wider poverty of the casualised, artisan and industrialised work-force, rather than professional beggars and vagrants. Nevertheless our contemporary appreciation of vagrancy as seen through the eyes of vagrants themselves is extended considerably by twentieth century sociologists, but at the expense of not locating their work in the context of a structural analysis of society.

The most complete history of vagrancy is to be found in Ribton-Turner's classic work entitled "A History of Vagrants and Vagrancy and Beggars and Begging" (Ribton-Turner, 1887). The earliest reference to the problem in the British Isles was in the Roman history of Ammianus Marcellus in A.D. 368 where the Scots were considered to be the majority of vagrants. References to vagrancy and vagrancy laws are to be found throughout Saxon times, but it is generally agreed amongst legal scholars that the first fully fledged vagrancy statute was passed in England in 1349, though this piece of legislation was preceded by earlier laws which served to lay the ground favourable to legislative innovation.

Ribton-Turner's analysis examined historically and socially the "homeless wanderer, and the beggar and vagabond" within a discussion of the social structure of early England, moving on to a detailed examination of vagrancy as reflected in the laws of the British Isles. Vagrancy is viewed as a history of economic and social oppression—a far cry from today's focus—in which labourers were pushed into a nomadic life-style through the need by landed and commercial interests for a cheap, mobile labour force. We thus have the beginnings of a full theory of vagrancy—however inarticulate—without the author having received the advantages of a radical sociological theorising.

It is precisely on this point that Chambliss (1964) takes forward our comprehension of the problem by anchoring his analysis within a sociology of law perspective. In selecting the legislative expression of vagrancy as the issue for investigation, he is explicitly concerned with the links between particular laws and the social setting in which these laws emerge, are interpreted and take form. Observing and explaining legislative changes by showing how they are related to the wider social structure reveals the interconnections between specific legal categories and society.

Basically, Chambliss (1964) is able to demonstrate that vagrancy statutes emerged for fundamentally economic reasons, namely the impact that the Black Death in 1348 had in decimating the labour force in an economy highly dependent on a ready supply of cheap labour. The vagrancy statutes of 1349 were thus designed to force labourers to take on employment at a low wage in order to ensure landowners a supply of labour at a price they could afford. Of course the Black Death was not the only force resulting in the emergence of vagrancy laws. Pound (1971) points to a number of other factors: the demobilisation of soldiers after the Wars of the Roses, the rising population, unemployment and economic depression arising out of the fall in the demand for textiles, inflation, the enclosure of common agricultural land, harvest failures, and the dissolution of the monasteries, all contributed to the problem of vagrancy and poverty to a greater or lesser extent. These factors acted independently and in conjunction. Their impact was either localised or national, sometimes extending over several decades. Put together, these factors, above all in their impact on the economy, were sufficient to cause considerable concern to successive Tudor governments.

Following a period of dormancy (the 1349 Act appears to have been fairly inconsequential in its effects) the vagrancy statutes take on a new focus of concern. The economic justification for the Act is now replaced by a concern with the criminal activities of vagrants. This new dimension becomes apparent in 1530, but especially in 1535, when the control of felons (persons who repeat the crime of vagrancy) as opposed to the movement of labourers, becomes the prime target for control. The new laws were explicitly designed to protect the property of commercial travellers in a society increasingly developing its commercial and industrial infra-structures. Thus although retaining its connections with economic factors, the emphasis of new legislation is with the criminal, not the economic activities of vagrants.

The consolidation of vagrancy statutes in terms of categories of criminal behaviour initiated in 1530 is achieved in the 1743 vagrancy statutes. Chambliss (1971, p. 72) claims that this function of the law on vagrancy

> has apparently continued through to the present day in England. The changes from 1743 to the present have been all in the direction of clarifying or expanding the categories covered, but little has been introduced to change either the meaning or the impact of this branch of law.

The contemporary attitude to vagrancy as exemplified by late nineteenth and twentieth century legislation, investigative commissions and social policy, suggests that the picture is somewhat more complex than Chambliss (1971) would suggest. The Vagrancy Acts of 1824 and 1935, particularly the former insofar as it is invoked to this day in Britain and is used primarily as a criminalising instrument by which to control vagrancy, remain actively on the statute books. Increasingly the focus of concern by legislators and policy makers is to redefine vagrancy in favour of a medical and social work strategy of control, and thereby replace the dominant criminal label attached to it.

The emergence of medicine and social work in the field of vagrancy—whereby vagrants became defined increasingly in the language of disease and social inadequacy—still carries with it the legacy of criminalising legislation (Archard, 1973). Thus society shows a confused response to vagrancy, at the one time handling him as an offender, ill or undersocialised. It is however the socio-medical conceptualisation and control of vagrancy that is striving to become the dominant paradigm by which we understand the problem. Consequently it is feasible that future legislation will reflect this redefinition over and against the criminalistic dimensions of the problem. Following Chambliss' thesis, what would be required of a contemporary analysis is investigating whether the emergence of this redefinition is connected with changes in the economic and social conditions of twentieth century Britain.

So far there has not been a specifically sociological study of legislation and social policy affecting vagrancy in the twentieth century. A study which explores the connections between economic and social structure, the extent and form of vagrancy, the ideology underpinning the development of the Welfare State, and the growing influence of medicine (especially psychiatry) and social work as practices seeking to redefine and control the problem, is required. A reading of the reports produced by central and local government departments, the social policy recommendations and legislation emanating from such reports, and the attempt by medicine and social work to include vagrancy within their domain of professional expertise, reveals a new focus of concern for the control of vagrancy (Archard, 1979).

What is apparent from literature on twentieth century vagrancy is the absence of any explanation about vagrancy and reaction to it, which explains the phenomenon within a framework such as the one suggested earlier. Our contemporary research strategy has been to study vagrants, not vagrancy. The research spy-glass is focused on the individual, not the social and political dimensions of the problem. The sociological study of legislation and policy, both at their ideological and institutional levels, has been forgotten. More significantly, the relationship between vagrancy, society's reaction to it, and the economic and social structure of contemporary capitalism, is absent in contemporary research. A closer examination of the literature cast in the mould of a crude empiricism will reveal these shortcomings.

Empiricist Accounts of Vagrancy

Surveys constitute the fundamental and almost exclusive tool of contemporary research on vagrants in Britain. Our understanding of the problem has been reduced to statistical and demographic distributions of the problem. Almost without exception, whether the rationale be the medical and social treatment, the social administration of the problem, or the extent of vagrancy in contemporary Britain, studies have been reduced to a crass empiricism, devoid of any articulate and specific theoretical framework.

There is no scope here to examine the intellectual forces behind the adoption of survey analysis as the dominant methodological tool with which to study social problems (Pinker, 1971). There are important theoretical, ideological and political influences which have resulted in the social sciences, particularly in Britain, taking on empiricism as a central method of analysis. Suffice it to say that surveys constitute very often both the means and the end of research into vagrants. Whether the survey is conducted by the research units of government departments or by individuals representing one or another profession seeking to treat or rehabilitate vagrants, the justification behind investigating the problem is the promotion and adoption of specific control ideas and practices bolstering strategies of treatment and rehabilitation. Little or no attention is paid to an objective analysis of those ideas and practices. Neither does the survey method in any way include either the relationship between vagrancy and its control, or historical and structural forces, at a societal level, as critically important factors determining the shape of vagrancy.

The central concern in this exploration of empirical accounts of vagrancy is two-fold: firstly, I wish to spell out what survey analysis tells us about vagrancy; secondly, I will outline what I see to be the connections between survey findings and the policy recommendations that are claimed to flow from them.

It has been the psychiatric profession and the social survey units of central government departments that have dominated work on the extent of vagrancy and the social and pathological characteristics of vagrants. Taking a lead from the social survey work of Booth (1901) and Rowntree (1901) on poverty in late nineteenth century urban Britain, government commissions of enquiry and the medical profession become interested in the aetiology of vagrancy by attempting to discover patterned characteristics in the employment, education, family background, sex, class and, above all, medical, psychological and social pathology of selected samples of vagrants (National Assistance Board, 1966; Wingfield-Digby, 1976; Tidmarsh and Wood, 1972; Sargaison, 1954; Wade, 1963; Lodge-Patch, 1970). Without exception these surveys focus on vagrants using common-lodging houses, government reception centres, mental hospitals, hostels and, to a lesser extent, vagrants found sleeping rough or in prison.

One major methodological problem the use of surveys as an adequate tool of enquiry presents investigators with, is the difficulty of obtaining a sample of vagrants which is representative of the total vagrant population. It has been widely recognised that institutions used by vagrants vary widely in terms of the needs they meet and the services they provide, such that statistically we are presented with variations as to the social and psychological pathology of populations in different institutions on which survey work has focused.

A second methodological problem is the lack of comparability between different surveys. The rationale behind the survey, the degree of comprehensiveness in the range of questions asked of vagrants, and the sophistication with which the data is analysed, all contribute to the lack of comparability.

A third problem of method, probably the most important since it challenges the scientific validity of many vagrancy surveys, is the self-fulfilling prophecy built into the surveys by the professional and correctionalist interests of the survey's advocates. This means that if psychiatrists, doctors and other para-medical professionals—such as psychiatric social workers—construct survey questionnaires to tease out the medical and psychological pathology of vagrants, then a level of pathology will be discovered. The very intervention of medicine into vagrancy, whether it is merely to investigate the problem or, as is more likely, to use the findings as a platform to advocate treatment and rehabilitation policy and practice, is likely to medicalise the problem. Consequently, the political result of medicalising vagrancy—or any social problem for that matter—is to redefine it in such a way that both historical and socio-economic factors, structurally understood, are considered peripheral or ignored altogether.

It is against this background that many investigators have concluded that the institutions vagrants use are, in the first and last analysis, the repository of a class of people who are there for reasons of physical and mental illness or social inadequacy, the victims of poor family background, crime, and inadequate social services. Poverty, unemployment or underemployment, homelessness, or the very impact that different methods of controlling vagrancy have in sustaining, rather than ameliorating the problem, are held to be insignificant. It is in this context, then, that common-lodging houses, hostels and reception centres—indeed all the institutions used by vagrants—came to be viewed as fulfilling the function of "an open asylum", a metaphor not accidental in its descriptive power.

Explanations for the continued existence of vagrancy rest upon an ideology which emphasises individual failure. This view is reflected in the method of survey questionnaires. By definition, questionnaires reduce the problem to individualistic interpretations of the phenomena. But, more significantly, because the medical and social work professions have begun to carve out a crucial role in the control of vagrancy, and their methods of treating social problems is highly individualised, the thrust of that investigative work is also designed to reflect personal dimensions of vagrancy. It is in this context that I argue that virtually all the research literature on vagrancy this century has been partial in its object and conclusions.

B

Given these limitations, what do empirical surveys tell us of the vagrant population? Two main issues constitute the focus behind most surveys on vagrants: they are the social and psychological factors individuals experience prior and subsequent to their arrival on skid row. The experience of a skid-row man in advance of his immersion into a vagrant life-style is held as relevant to the aetiology of homelessness and destitution; the symptoms of that life-style point to the solutions appropriate to his rehabilitation or treatment. Answers to these questions are often provided within a framework of demographic data pertaining to the survey population. The number, age, sex, class, marital status and employment profiles of vagrants reveal similarities in distinct survey samples drawn from various skid row institutions.

A detailed inspection of contemporary empirical surveys on the problem is not offered here. What I wish to outline are the demographic and statistical features of vagrancy in summary form, since the patterned similarities which emerge from them is immediately apparent. What is more important is an examination of the practical implications drawn from these studies, since I argue that the social policy strategies being currently promoted to tackle the problem do not always follow logically or scientifically from the data collected.

A comparison of surveys conducted on homeless persons living in common-lodging houses, reception centres, hostels, prisons, mental hospitals, or sleeping rough shows that around 90% of skid row consists of men (Tidmarsh and Wood, 1972). Over 70% are 40 years of age or more, while only 18% are married at the time of the surveys, the remainder being single, divorced or widowed. Of the surveys conducted in England only 56% of the respondents originated from England and Wales while 41% came from Scotland and Ireland. However, the proportion of English-born homeless men in Scottish and Irish common-lodging houses is less than 10%, thus pointing to migration as a significant factor in the make-up on the English skid row scene. At the time of the surveys the unemployment rate averaged 64%. In addition investigations have demonstrated that mental illness, personality disorder, physical disabilities and alcoholism are highly prevalent amongst the skid-row population. For instance, Tidmarsh and Wood (1972) showed that approximately 26% of their sample of 8000 men were alcoholics, 18% and 22% suffered from mental illnesses and personality disorders respectively, 7% experienced physical illnesses, epilepsy or old age and 27% were primarily in the centre for reasons of migration and employment.

In the eyes of most advocates of the survey method the demographic features and social and medical pathology constitute the specific character of the skid row population. It is the patterned occurrence of deprived backgrounds and deviant behaviour which consitutes the basis for promoting a a particular strategy of control towards the problem. Three major works— major in the sense that the scale of the surveys were much more comprehensive than the usual work done in this field—may be taken as indicative of policy developments in the field of the single homeless. These works are the National Assistance Board survey "Homeless Single Persons" (National Assistance Board, 1966), the study commissioned by the Department of Health and Social Security on the Camberwell Reception Centre (Tidmarsh and Wood, 1972) and "Hostels and Lodgings for Single People" (Wingfield-Digby, 1976), conducted by the government's Office of Population Censuses and Surveys.

It might be argued that the first and third of these studies are not explicitly concerned with the promotion of reform and rehabilitation policies, but merely state the statistical facts on vagrancy. Neither study sets out recommendations for tackling the problem, but both studies, like Tidmarsh and Wood (1972), underscore the deprivation, unemployment, institutionalisation, and both physical and mental ill-health of a population evidently trapped in a closed circuit of common-lodging houses, hostels, reception centres, hospitals, prisons and sleeping rough. In the context of these features the overall strategy consists of decriminalising vagrancy, introducing medical and social care and rehabilitation, advocating the establishment of small-scale rehabilitation hostels as replacement to the impersonal human warehouses, prisons, mental hospitals, common-lodging houses—in short, incorporating the single homeless into the welfare provision of a system underpinned by an ethic of individual care and treatment.

From the standpoint of social policy formulation the major value of surveys on the single homeless is that they are used as evidence for justifying policies which direct attention at the social and medical pathology of the individual. Thus government policy documents such as "Habitual Drunken Offenders" (Home Office, 1971), and policy circulars on homelessness, alcoholism and mental illness (Department of the Environment (DoE) and Department of Health and Social Security (DHSS), 1974; DHSS, 1972; DHSS, 1973) are promoted in the light of the conclusions arrived at by such surveys. The link between survey material and social policy prescription is brought together in its clearest form in the study by Tidmarsh and Wood (1972). In their conclusion they recommend that the Department of Health and Social Security, the Department of the Environment, Regional Hospital Boards, Local Authorities, the Home Office, and private, commercial and voluntary agencies should offer more extensive and improved treatment, rehabilitative and after-care services. They ask that these services continuously monitor the personal needs of the single homeless population, and test their effectiveness in achieving the primary objective of these services, namely the resettlement and reintegration of single homeless persons into mainstream society.

There is, of course, no scientific evidence that such policies flow from the survey findings. The call for improved and more extensive after-care services, for instance, is a reflection of the power of specific professions, such as medicine, psychiatry and social work, to impose their professional beliefs and definitions on the problem. This is a political and ideological process involving the ascendancy of specific conceptual categories and methods of operating towards vagrancy. Moreover, the framework invoked by these professions to conceptualise the single homeless, ignores both structural and institutional forces serving to generate and sustain the problem. They fail to recognise the interrelationship between the manifestation of the problem and attempts at controlling it. No attempt is made to grasp the impact that correctional policies have in confirming the status and problems of the single homeless to the point where such policies themselves have an iatrogenic power. Above all, the conceptual framework of psychiatry and social work, in reducing the problem to the statistical distribution of personal pathology and particular methods of care, denies the central meanings that vagrants give to correctional agencies, and isolates them from the wider society of which the problem is an integral part. It is the meaning of skid row, both for its inhabitants and professionals working with them, that constitutes the focus of research employing naturalism as a method of enquiry.

Naturalistic Accounts of Vagrancy

"The Hobo: The Sociology of the Homeless Man" (Anderson, 1923), is a classic study of the subculture of migrant workers in the United States. This study marks a radical departure from orthodox theorising and methods on social problems. In sharp contrast to the kind of empirical surveys mentioned above, in which investigators bring their own professional interests to their researches, Anderson's point of departure for analysing hoboes is the point of view of the subject himself. Here we have an attempt to give the subject an authentic voice in his deviant enterprise. A naturalistic perspective permits the hobo or vagrant to express the essential meaning homelessness, institutionalisation and vagrancy has for him, seen through his own eyes rather than through the perspective of medicine, social work or law-enforcement.

I wish to dwell for a moment on this perspective because of its implications for how we understand and respond to the problem of vagrancy.

The essential feature of studies stressing the subjective perspective of the actors under study is the social realism with which deviants of one kind or another are portrayed. In these studies the subjects often come to life, revealing a complex and sophisticated pattern of values and practices which reflect the skills human beings develop in order to survive the iniquities of deprivation, oppression and poverty. But it is these very skills and values, in their immediacy and arising out of the concrete, everyday situations experienced by deviants, rather than their location in the overall social structure, which are highlighted by such studies. The reason for this emphasis is that investigators adopting a naturalistic perspective and method seek to immerse themselves in the life-style of their research subjects. The purpose is to study deviants in their own natural settings, observing and grasping the inner structures of their life-styles as they unfold on a daily basis (Matza, 1969).

The tradition that the Chicago School of Sociology of the 1920s established in studying deviant and ethnic subcultures from the inside (Nels Anderson was part of this tradition) eventually fell into disuse. However it was revived in the 1960s in the United States of America, particularly through a perspective entitled symbolic interactionism, a perspective seeking to understand the subjective meaning of deviancy held by the incumbents immersed in it (Becker, 1963; Rubington and Weinberg, 1968). A number of studies have now been published in the United States stressing the ethnographic and subjective dimensions of life on skid row. The four most significant are Spradley (1970), Straus (1974), Wiseman (1971) and Wallace (1958).

Each of these studies gives detailed and vivid inside accounts of vagrancy, alcoholism and institutionalisation. Although aware of the severe deprivations homeless men undergo, nevertheless what becomes evident from these studies is the essential humanity retained by persons confronted by homelessness, disease, unemployment and poverty. In addition, and this is particularly true of Wiseman (1971), the analysis includes an appreciation of the impact that various forms of social control have on homeless men, and has the distinct advantage over previous work, whether in the naturalistic vein or not, of juxtaposing an analysis of homeless men with that of the theory, ideology and practice of social control agents and the institutions they work for. In her study a careful and detailed account is offered of the contradictory and overlapping definitions held by alcoholics and social control agents.

Devoid of the arid statistical analysis of empiricist surveys, the naturalistic work of an American sociologist looking at the skid row phenomenon stresses a critically important dimension which most investigative work in sociology misses out on: the social meaning of life on skid row, whether it be viewed from the standpoint of the homeless man or that of the various professions working with them in an institutional setting.

Unfortunately the resurgence of a naturalistic perspective in America has not resulted in any extensive work on vagrancy being similarly done in Great Britain, apart from Archard (1979), where I attempt an analysis of the relationship between deviancy and social control in terms of interpersonal, institutional and ideological forces affecting both homeless alcoholics and professionals working with them.

In spite of my efforts to locate what everyday life for homeless alcoholics and agents of social control means from their own respective standpoints in the context of a broader analysis of shifts in criminal, social and medical policy, the study fails to achieve the objectives of a full theory of vagrancy. The study is neither adequately informed historically, nor does it set out to locate vagrancy and alcoholism structurally by pointing to the relationship it has to the inequitable distribution of power, wealth and other resources in the wider social system. This in fact is a common weakness of naturalistic analysis. It assumes the experiences of its subjects to constitute an awareness of their immediate social situation as if they were unconnected and un-influenced by wider determining social, economic and political forces.

Naturalism as a perspective disqualifies the investigator from asking the kind of questions posed at the beginning of this paper. Instead, studying specific subcultural formations and reactions to them, the naturalistic perspective often falsely humanises the deviant enterprise while misdirecting its criticism at the impact of social workers, law-enforcement officers and psychiatrists in labelling homeless men and thereby confirming their deviant identity (Gouldner, 1973).

Conclusion

The problem of skid row, then, is not merely the summation of the individual characteristics of homeless men differentiating them from the general popu-lation, as empirical surveys would have it. But neither is it the subjective definitions of deviants and professionals working with them or seeking to control the problem in terms of social policy formulations. The significance of empiricism for social policy makers has been to expand and increase the intervention of professionals into new areas of social control, while at the same time remaining uncritical of the very nature of such intervention, treating it as if it were not a crucial feature of the problem itself. Naturalism, on the other hand, has romanticised vagrant life-styles, on occasions ignoring the relationship it has to agencies of social control. Where it does focus on this relationship, however, it tends to offer a misplaced critique of the re-formism of professional practice, as if practitioners themselves were isolated from wider structural and ideological shifts in society's reaction to social problems. Historical accounts do, instead, identify those very structural and ideological dimensions, but fail to illustrate how they are mediated through institutional arrangements such that they are shown to have a concrete im-pact on everyday life. What is now required is a more comprehensive, dia-lectical study of vagrancy, social control, and society, along the lines specified in the earlier part of this review. It must be a study which points to the neces-sity for widespread changes in society while at the same time indicating how the problem of vagrancy may be tackled radically in the immediate future, at the level of abolishing the dehumanising laws and institutional arrangements which serve to perpetuate the problem.

References

Anderson, N. (1923). "The Hobo: The Sociology of the Homeless Man." University of Chicago Press, Chicago.

Archard, P. (1973). Sad, bad or mad: society's confused response to the skid row alcoholic. *In* "Contemporary Social Problems in Britain" (Bailey, R. and Young, J., eds). D. C. Heath, Farnborough.

Archard, P. (1979). "Vagrancy, Alcoholism and Social Control." Macmillan, London.

Becker, H. (1963). "Outsiders: Studies in the Sociology of Deviance." Free Press, New York.

Booth, C. (1901). "Life and Labour of the People in London", 3rd edition. Macmillan, London.

Booth, W. (1890). "In Darkest England and the Way Out." Salvation Army, London.

Chambliss, W. J. (1964). A sociological analysis of the law on vagrancy. *Soc. Prob.* **12**, 66–77.

Cohen, S. (1974). Criminology and the sociology of deviance in Britain. *In* "Deviance and Social Control" (Rock, P. and McIntosh, M., eds). Tavistock Publications, London.

Cohen, S. (1975). It's alright for you to talk: political and sociological manifestos for social action. *In* "Radical Social Work" (Bailey, R. and Brake, M., eds). Edward Arnold, London.

Crossley, B. and Denmark, J. C. (1969). Community care: a study of the psychiatric morbidity of a Salvation Army hostel. *Br. J. Sociol.* **20** (4), 443–449.

Davies, W. H. (1971). "The Autobiography of a Super Tramp." Jonathan Cape, London.

Department of the Environment and Department of Health and Social Security (1974). "Homelessness", Joint Circulars 18/74 and 4/74. HMSO, London.

Department of Health and Social Security (1972). "Homeless Single Persons in Need of Care and Support", Circular 37/72. HMSO, London.

Department of Health and Social Security (1973). "Community Services for Alcoholics", Circular 21/73. HMSO, London.

Edwards, G., Hawker, A., Williamson, A. and Hensman, C. (1966). London's skid row. *Lancet*, **1**, 249–252.

Gouldner, A. (1973). The sociologist as partisan: sociology and the welfare state. *In* "For Sociology". Penguin, Harmondsworth.

Home Office (1971). "Habitual Drunken Offenders." HMSO, London.

Laidlaw, J. (1966). "Glasgow Common Lodging Houses and the People Living in Them." Health and Welfare Committee, Glasgow Corporation.

Lodge-Patch, I. C. (1970). Homeless men—a London survey. *Proc. R. Coll. Med.* **63**, 437–441.

Matza, D. (1969). "Becoming Deviant." Prentice-Hall, New Jersey.

National Assistance Board (1966). "Homeless Single Persons." HMSO, London.

O'Connor, P. (1963). "Vagrancy." Penguin, Harmondsworth.

Orwell, G. (1949). "Down and Out in Paris and London." Penguin, Harmondsworth.

Pinker, R. (1971). "Social Theory and Social Policy." Heinemann, London.

Pound, J. (1971). "Poverty and Vagrancy in Tudor England." Longman, London.

Ribton-Turner, C. J. (1887). "A History of Vagrants and Vagrancy and Beggars and Begging." Chapman and Hall, London.

Rowntree, S. (1901). "Poverty, A Study of Town Life." Macmillan, London.

Rubington, E. and Weinberg, M. (eds) (1968). "Deviance: The Interactionist Perspective." Macmillan, London.

Sandford, J. (1971). "Down and Out in Britain." Peter Owen, London.

Sargaison, E. (1954). "Growing Old in Common Lodgings." Nuffield Provincial Hospitals Trust, London.

Smart, W. J. (1935). "Christ of the Thames Embankment." Hodder and Stoughton, London.

Spradley, J. (1970). "You Owe Yourself a Drunk: An Ethnology of Urban Nomads." Little, Brown, Boston.

Straus, R. (1974). "Escape from Custody." Harper and Row, New York.

Tidmarsh, D. and Wood, S. M. (1972). "Camberwell Reception Centre; Summary of Research Findings and Recommendations." Department of Health and Social Security, London.

Wade, C. C. (1963). Survey of inmates of a common lodging house. *Med. Officer*, **109**, 171–173.

Wallace, S. (1958). "Skid Row as a Way of Life." Bedminster Press, New Jersey.

Wingfield-Digby, P. (1976). "Hostels and Lodgings for Single People." HMSO, London.

Wiseman, J. (1971). "Stations of the Lost: The Treatment of Skid Row Alcoholics." Prentice-Hall, New Jersey.

Dossers and Jake Drinkers: The View from One End of Skid Row

PETER PHILLIMORE

Introduction

This article is about the ways in which one section of a skid-row population in the Spitalfields area of London identify themselves and their fellows on skid row.* Vagrants, or dossers, as many prefer to call themselves, are usually classified on grounds which are relevant to a variety of organisations which have dealings with them. For instance, courts, prisons, hospitals and social work agencies tend to separate vagrant alcoholics from those who are considered to be mentally ill, while those with a professional interest in vagrant alcoholics would in many contexts make further distinctions. As one would expect, the greater the professional involvement with vagrants the more refinements are introduced to differentiate between them. Such distinctions are drawn, however, without reference to the manner in which the men on skid row define each other; and differences between themselves which these men perceive to be important are not likely to be a matter of consideration for the agencies which deal with them. I am interested, then, in the differences which one group of dossers recognise among themselves and among the wider skid-row population, and how this is reflected in the terms of identity they use. This leads me to look at the ways in which they organise certain

---

* The research on which this article is based was conducted over a three-month period while studying for an M.A. in Social Anthropology at Edinburgh University. This was a Participant Observation Study using unstructured methods, and based on simply frequenting the Spitalfields Market area at all times of the day or night, although the most fruitful period was between 7 p.m. and 7 a.m.

aspects of their daily lives, and the part played by their social distinctions in these contexts.

The subjects of this study cannot be considered representative of skid row in general, nor are they readily classified in the typologies of the agencies which have dealings with vagrants, except that they may be defined negatively as neither alcoholic nor mentally ill. My original intention had been to study those who did casual work at Spitalfields Market. This proved a convenient way to start for it was easy to locate a number of men who undertook casual work. If an outsider's perspective were adopted, it would be possible for the observer to impose the identity of "casual workers" on these men, and to treat them accordingly as a distinct body of people. But it soon became apparent that those who did casual work at Spitalfields Market saw themselves as a distinct group in a restricted and fairly unimportant way. Instead they identified themselves as part of a broader category of people, among whom only a proportion did casual work, and for whom such work was by no means a necessary defining feature of their identity. In this chapter I look at this as yet unnamed wider category.

Spitalfields Market is situated on the edge of an area approximately one mile square which contains many locales frequented by vagrants. Whitechapel, Aldgate, Brick Lane and Cable Street, besides Spitalfields, are focal points of their world within a very small area of the East End of London. Indeed, while it is said that skid row as a geographical phenomenon does not exist in this country, that there is not the same concentration of vagrants' social institutions here as is found in some North American cities, a strong case could be made for exempting from this generalisation the area around Spitalfields.

Social Identification

I have already mentioned the word "dosser" to describe people who are often referred to by external agencies as vagrants or the single homeless. "Dosser" is widely favoured as an indigenous term of identity among skid-row men in general, but for those men who are the subjects of study here it is *the* term of identity. They describe themselves as dossers, and to use the term of someone else is to acknowledge a similarity and identity with him: a dosser is someone like oneself, and in this way the term "dosser" can denote a wider or narrower circle of skid-row men, according to the needs of the context. This last comment is important, for dossers constantly redefine each other and, indeed, all the vagrants in the area, from one situation to another. Such redefinition oscillates typically between recognition of another person as a dosser, and their relegation to another category, that of "jake-drinker". This latter, or its variant forms of "jack-drinker" and "jake-wallah", is a label which carries distinctly pejorative implications. No dosser would accept the term as a description of himself, but equally none would hesitate to impose it on other dossers from whom he wished to disassociate himself in a particular situation.

"Dosser" and "jake-drinker" are the most important social categories among the men whom I studied. It must be understood, nevertheless, that these terms do not isolate empirically distinguishable groups. Not only do definitions as to which men are dossers and which are jake-drinkers vary from person to person, but the same dosser will classify in a different fashion in a different situation, as I hope to show later. Likewise, there is no clear-cut boundary which separates dossers from members of the wider society, and a few individuals occupy an ambiguous position on the margins of the dossers' world: sometimes classed by others as dossers, sometimes not, they express similar ambivalence in the way they regard themselves. There is nothing surprising in this. Social identities, like all categories, have a dual significance, being imposed on experience in order to shape, and hence control it, as well as purporting to reflect this experience. Nevertheless, a striking feature of dossers' social relations is the lack of standardisation in the way they classify each other, and the lack of concordance between categories and empirically isolable groups.

What, then, are the criteria according to which men are defined as dossers, and what are considered to be the characteristics of jake-drinkers? Dossers are, to varying degrees, familiar with definitions of themselves in terms of their homelessness, their lack of a regular job, and their records of imprisonment for minor offences, Such criteria make up the picture of dossers as socially inadequate and psychologically unstable, conceptions which are grounded in the aetiological concerns of agencies with a professional involvement with dossers. It is through their encounters with these agencies, both punitive and rehabilitative, that dossers have become familiar with their identification in these terms. The habitual, automatic way in which dossers characterise each other, however, is very different. For them, familiarity with a range of social situations, and knowledge of strategies for "making out" in the world, indicate whether or not someone is a dosser. A number of these social situations comprise formal, institutional provision for the skid-row man. Foremost among these are places of shelter: the "sally" (Salvation Army hostels), "Rowtons" (a kind of cheap commercial hotel), common-lodging houses, the "spike" (Government Reception Centre) and night shelters run by voluntary agencies. As well as places which offer shelter, there are a handful of institutions which offer cash, food and clothing to dossers; "hand-outs" are run by a variety of charitable bodies, such as ex-servicemen's welfare organisations and church missions. But besides institutions specifically directed towards the dosser, there is a further range of situations which arise out of a redefinition by dossers of the physical world which they share with everyone else in the wider society. Parks, railway stations, cafés, pubs and off-licences take on a fresh significance for dossers which centres on the question of how much they are able to carry on their way of life without arousing hostility and harassment which would make use of these facilities impossible. In the same way, when a dosser talks of "skippers" or "skippering" he is redefining a derelict building or some other physical location as a source of shelter and a place to sleep. In the context of this article there are two specific settings of importance to dossers: Spitalfields Market is a source of casual work; while the open fire across the yard from the entrance to the market is a focal point and gathering place for dossers in the vicinity of Spitalfields.

The strategies for making out clearly include knowing how to handle effectively the situations I have just mentioned. Considerable energy is expended in working out the most fruitful ways to exploit a situation, and the knowledge which dossers hold about different aspects of their world testifies to the purposefulness and the degree of organisation which goes into the business of living. Money-making strategies are of almost infinite variety: doing casual work in the market at Spitalfields represents merely one source of casual work among several in the locality, although it does provide the greatest number of opportunities. Two local street markets take on small gangs of casual workers to set up and to dismantle the stalls; some nearby clothes factories are reputed to provide casual work opportunities packing off-cuts; occasionally there is work to be had with local firms helping to load and unload lorries; while ways to obtain kitchen-portering jobs are usually known about. But there are many dossers who rarely, if ever, undertake casual work, throwing an added emphasis on other money-making strategies, such as different types of begging (Orwell, 1966; Archard, 1975), making the rounds of hand-outs, attempting to claim money off the state through the Department of Health and Social Security, or in some cases small-scale thieving (Archard, 1975).

For one dosser to describe another man as a dosser is to ignore differences between them, or at least to recognise that what contrasts them is for the present less important than what they have in common. Thus the term "dosser" can be employed to extend over the entire skid-row population in one context, or in another situation it can be contracted to denote a small collection of people. The term "jake-drinker" is used with comparable flexibility but with contrasting intentions. To describe someone as a jake-drinker is to reclassify them and to dwell on differences which are perceived to exist or are imputed to the man in question. A jake-drinker is literally someone who drinks the jake or the jack, the indigenous terms for crude spirits. However, among the subjects of this study the term is frequently generalised, so that a dosser may describe any number of fellow dossers as jake-drinkers if he should wish to differentiate himself from them at a particular moment. In consequence, while dossers will describe jake-drinkers as "the blokes who drink the jack" if the question is put to them, in practice many of them use the term in a partly pitying, partly abusive fashion to separate themselves from those they consider to be in a worse state. What counts as a worse state is clearly going to vary. For the dosser who obtains casual work on a fairly regular basis, always has some money on him, eats regularly, drinks in pubs and sleeps in a good skipper, most remaining dossers are liable to be dismissed as jake-drinkers from time to time. But for others who make out in the world less successfully, or for alcoholics who drink cheap wine and cider, the term "jake-drinker" is likely to be used in a way which corresponds more to the literal meaning of the word.

I have already remarked that no dosser would accept a description of himself as a jake-drinker.* The usual reaction of those who are labelled in this way is to deny that there is any difference between themselves and the dossers who so discredit them. "We're all dossers here" is a recurring motif of much of dossers' social relations, and an inevitable corollary of the processes of social differentiation by which individual dossers attempt to assert a superior status. In such contexts those who are designated inferior usually refuse to recognise the proposed definition of the situation by reasserting that they are all equal, and possibly by adding that the "real" jake-drinkers are yet another group.

Among the subjects of this study "dosser" and "jake-drinker" are the crucial social categories. But two further terms of identity must be mentioned, "nutters" and "casuals". "Nutters" is employed in a way which complements the usage of "jake-drinkers"—a pejorative term by which the mentally ill among skid-row habitués are dismissed, but also an inviting term of abuse for more general use. It is not, however, an important social category in the same way that "jake-drinkers" is. The additional term of identity had some relevance in the context of the Spitalfields locality but is not of general significance: that is, the men who seek casual work at Spitalfields Market and are sometimes referred to collectively as "casuals" and describe themselves in the same way. The term is by no means used by all dossers, and, for those who do use it, it is restricted to those occasions when dossers are actually engaged in looking for casual work at the entrance to the market. The various casual work outlets outside the Spitalfields Market have no term of identity associated with them: a dosser may have a regular casual job in one of the neighbouring street markets but he does not thereby become a casual. The use of terms of identity to discriminate between themselves does not exhaust the

---

* It needs to be stressed that this article is about one section of the wider skid-row population, and in overall respects the findings reported here may well not apply elsewhere on skid-row. For example, Archard (1975), in his fieldwork among alcoholic dossers indicates that there are striking differences between the men studied here and alcoholics in the forms of social relationships and in the differing interpretations, for instance, of social categories such as "dosser" and "jake-drinker".

possibilities dossers have for drawing such distinctions. In any setting dossers find ways of exploiting the situation in order to project themselves as superior to those with whom they interact. For instance while dossers who are engaged in casual work at Spitalfields Market repeatedly voice the opinion that they are superior to other dossers, and often label those around the fire as jake-drinkers, a parallel process continues all the time among the men at the market entrance without the participants having recourse to social categories to express their distinctions. In a word, social distinctions operate at every level, down to contrasts which seem minute to the outsider.

Social Situations within the Dosser's World

I intend now to examine the ways in which social categorisation operates in practice in particular social situations. I shall look first at the process of obtaining work at Spitalfields Market. Secondly, I shall discuss patterns of behaviour around the open fire opposite the market. This part of the article will be concluded with a section on behaviour in skippers.

Casual Work at Spitalfields Market

Spitalfields Market provides dossers with an important source of money, taking casual jobs offered to them by drivers who are delivering produce to the market and who want some help unloading their lorries. Because dossers gather at the entrance to the market to await the arrival of the lorries, the market entrance is a significant focal point for dossers' interaction among themselves.* Casual work can be obtained in the market, six days a week between 4 or 5 p.m. and about 4 a.m. However, the vast majority of deliveries occur between 10 p.m. and 2 a.m., and this is the time when dossers congregate in any numbers around the entrance to the market. There are rarely more than six or seven at the entrance at any one time, but typically between ten and twenty spend some time waiting for work in the course of a night. Before this time there may be two or three waiting for work; usually these are men who have regular arrangements with drivers whom they know to be delivering produce early. After 4 a.m. the stall-holders and porters arrive, followed by the buyers, and the dossers make themselves scarce, for the presence of the porters precludes the possibility of the dossers finding work.

---

* Throughout the passage on Spitalfields Market I use the terms "dossers" and "casuals" interchangeably to denote the men engaged in looking for work at the market.

I mentioned above that dossers who are seeking work at the market regard themselves as better off in every way than those who stand around the fire which is visible across the yard in front of the market entrance. This view persists in spite of the fact that there is some interchange between the two places, as men go to and fro, perhaps to wait for the soup-run at the fire, or to warm themselves between jobs or to chat with others they know. Indeed, what is being expressed is a conceptual contrast between two milieux, both of which have considerable importance to dossers, even though the men at the market condemn those at the fire as a bunch of jake-drinkers.

One dimension of this contrast is to be found in the position of casuals *vis-à-vis* the police and the Beadles (market security employees). Dossers believe that they are fairly safe from police harassment when they are at the market looking for work. Whereas the fire is seen to be a hazardous place which attracts unceasing police attention, the market entrance is believed to have something of a sanctuary value. "At least they won't come bothering us here" is a frequently heard remark when the casuals see the police at the fire. This attitude is based partly on the expectation that the Beadles will intercede on the casuals' behalf if necessary, because being in the market they come under the authority of the market security. A further consideration, however, is that in seeking work, casuals believe they attain a social legitimacy which distinguishes them from the attentions of the latter. Indeed, this assessment of the situation is obviously shared by some of the dossers who never come to the market looking for work, for it is not uncommon to see men making their way from the fire to the market entrance at the first sign of, or in anticipation of, trouble with the police. Their assessment is well-founded, but dossers remain cautious for they point out that although the police may leave them alone by and large at the market entrance they nevertheless keep an eye on the market and are always liable to make a visit. When the police arrive at the fire to extinguish it and to disperse the dossers assembled there, the men at the market often express their sympathy. Yet their comparative safety contrasted with the vulnerability of the dossers at the fire provides them, from their own standpoint, with a further index of their superior status. The fact that casuals are under the authority of the more benign Beadles has more than just instrumental value; it marks their difference from the dossers at the fire, and indicates the gap between them. The fire is a place subject to police control, the market is subject to control by its own security personnel.

Differences among the men at the market entrance are most clearly revealed in the different attitudes displayed towards the actual business of obtaining work. A number of men express the view that casuals should never ask drivers for jobs, and should wait till the driver approaches them. They should then discover what the driver intends to pay them and what the job entails (for instance, how many boxes, or sacks, what type of produce, and where the deliveries are to be made). When he knows the answers to these questions he can decide whether or not he wants the job. The reasons given for the need to negotiate are that it is important to show the driver that the relationship is on an equal footing, that you are doing him as much of a favour by working for him as he is by taking you on, and that you do not expect to be treated as cheap, exploitable labour. "Give the drivers half a chance", these casuals say, "and they will treat you like dirt". By asking how much you are going to be paid you can ensure that you receive a fair rate for the job. If a dosser asks a driver for a job, or takes on work without discovering how much he is going to earn, he is at the driver's mercy. Were this simply a matter between an individual dosser and a driver there would be no cause for other dossers to be concerned. But if drivers know that there are dossers who will "crawl" for jobs, or who will work for a pittance, then drivers will be able to pay less than a decent rate all the time, which would be a matter of concern for all dossers who do casual work.

Yet although there is muted acknowledgement of the sense of this approach the majority of dossers who seek casual work voice a different argument. Less eloquently than the few mentioned above they take the view that "we're dossers: we can't afford to pick and choose". They emphasise the competitiveness of the casual work scene, and regard enquiring how much the driver intends to pay them as a futile gesture which merely encourages the driver to look elsewhere for help. It is not that they have any illusions about the drivers' generosity, but rather that they know their own negotiating position to be a weak one, with almost any work being preferable to none at all.

The disparity between these two approaches tends to reflect the difference between dossers who do casual work regularly and those who turn up at the market on an intermittent basis. For the more regular workers are likely to develop links with particular drivers who hire them whenever they deliver to the market. Such regular contacts are usually better paid than the jobs obtained on a completely *ad hoc* basis, and they also provide a modicum of financial security which enables these men to articulate with confidence the approach towards obtaining work which I documented above. Regular contacts with drivers also make it easier for a dosser to sustain the notion of an equal relationship with drivers, which is such a bone of contention between dossers. Going over to talk to a driver, instead of being condemned as "crawling" for a job, is projected as—although not always recognised as— chatting to a mate. Lorry drivers are not a part of the social milieu of most dossers, so it is not surprising to find that those few dossers who are able to, exploit their contacts to suggest that they are not really dossers at all. This is a complex topic, and I discuss its ramifications in greater detail below. In a similar manner, regular appearance at the market enables certain dossers to suggest that they are on terms of easy familiarity with the Beadles, and can even count on their assistance in finding jobs.

The notion of an equal relationship with drivers cannot be sustained without bargaining with them, and no dosser contemplates this course of action without the security of knowing that he has the chance to earn money from other, regular sources. Yet while the bulk of dossers who obtain casual work might like to suggest that their contacts with drivers are on an equal footing, the immediate necessity to earn some money, and the constant indications that the drivers do not look on the relationship as an equal one, bring home to them how unbalanced it is, and nourish the resentment which they feel towards the drivers.

The regularity of casual work at the market, and the ensuing contacts with drivers which this brings, is thus the factor which most influences social categorisation in this setting. Those who scramble for jobs regardless of any ideal code of behaviour, and who recognise, perhaps grudgingly, that "we're dossers, and it's no use being choosy", find it difficult to dispute that the men who have a regular source of money from casual work are in a more fortunate position than themselves. They will never allow, however, that these others are not dossers, which, as I have indicated above, is the claim that the latter sometimes make. These few talk about their particular approach to obtaining jobs in the full knowledge that the majority of dossers will not be able to act in this fashion, and that their own ability to act in this way gives them the means to indicate their own superior status. Likewise, although they exhort the other dossers to make sure that the drivers treat them as equals, and not as exploitable, cheap labour, in practice the manifest imbalance in the relationships between most dossers and drivers suits them well, and is fodder for their claim that they are not dossers at all. For they are able to differentiate themselves from the majority of dossers by taking the status of relationships with drivers as a yardstick for determining whether or not someone is a dosser; in other words, if your contacts with drivers are minimal and unequal then you are by definition a dosser. Furthermore, the very fact of working to obtain money gives those who do casual work a higher status than other dossers, in their own eyes (predictably those who obtain money in other ways despise those who work for money, or at least they affect to do so). Consequently, the more a man works in the market the more he can lay claim to an important indicator of a position in the wider society.

It might be argued that certain of the men who take casual jobs at the market are not dossers at all. Certainly it would be true to say that occasionally men appear who are unambiguously not skid-row figures: for instance, men who may be temporarily unemployed. A handful of others who frequent the market are on the margins of the dossers' world, their position ambiguous to other dossers and even to themselves. A man who owns a car, even if it is untaxed and not roadworthy; or a man who turns up at the market one night looking for work and another day drives a lorry, offering casual employment himself; such men are not easily classified, and are held in some suspicion by other dossers. However there are no more than three or four men in this position, and, discounting these few, the bulk of the dossers who spend time at the market entrance have no hesitation in refusing to accept the definition of themselves put forward by some other casuals who imply that because they maintain regular contacts with certain drivers they are not dossers at all. The view of the majority is that these views represent a vain attempt by some to convince themselves and others that they are *not* dossers, when really they and everyone else know that they are. There is a further justification for agreeing here with the majority of the casuals. Some of their fellow casuals do try to exploit personal indicators of a position in the wider society, but the audience before whom they endeavour to carve out this non-dosser identity consists of other dossers. It is clearly helpful to a dosser that a driver who employs him regularly should differentiate him from the other dossers at the market (although whether or not drivers actually do so is another matter). But the significance of a dossers' actions is intended above all to be understood by other dossers, and some go to considerable lengths to make sure that these actions are witnessed. These actions do not always have a direct connection with the workings of the market and the process of obtaining casual work, but the audience of dossers at the market entrance and the proximity of the fire with a further audience makes the yard in front of the market a favourite stage. One of the regular casuals won £60 on the horses. He bought himself a new suit, shirt, tie and shoes, had a haircut, and then ordered a taxi to pick up himself and two others at the market entrance to take them to the dog races. The audience, and the reaction of the other dossers, was all important; there could be no question of walking to the nearest busy street and hailing a taxi without dossers being witness to the scene. Nevertheless, other dossers did not respond as they were intended to; instead of recognising that the threesome could hardly be dossers if they behaved in this fashion, the prevailing view took the form of "what a laugh to think of three dossers going off in a taxi". They may be behaving in an unusual fashion but they were dossers none the less.

The Spitalfields Fire

The fire at Spitalfields is the only one of its kind in London: a regular open fire. It is lit and maintained by dossers, using chiefly the wooden debris from the market. In winter attempts may be made to light the fire during the day, but usually it is lit at some point in the evening, when one or two dossers wander over to the site carrying wooden boxes and light the fire. Gradually other dossers appear. The busiest time at the fire corresponds to the busiest time at the market entrance for those dossers who are looking for casual work: between 10 p.m. and 2 a.m. Numbers vary greatly, but at the peak, waiting for the soup-run to arrive, there may be as many as fifty dossers present, although the average is around twenty to thirty. With the arrival of the soup further dossers appear, and there is a brief exodus from the market entrance.

There is some considerable coming and going in the hours before the soup-run appears. Small groups talking and arguing coalesce and fragment endlessly. After the soup the numbers at the fire diminish, as dossers disperse to seek work, to go to their skippers, or wander away. Those remaining have no skippers and are not looking for work. They are usually quieter now, some of them stretched out asleep, others standing facing alternately towards and away from the fire as they warm first their fronts and then their backs. A group may be drinking together. The fire is kept alight in a desultory fashion. Until 4 a.m. the numbers at the fire remain stable, and then more departures reduce numbers to barely two or three. This occurs because the Salvation Army hostel nearby opens its doors to allow dossers to snatch a couple of hours' sleep on chairs or benches, and most of the men still around the fire make use of this opportunity.

From 4 a.m. onwards, then, the fire dies out and ceases to be a focal point for dossers. A further reason inhibits its use after 4.30 a.m.: the market comes to life, and all the space in the yard in front of the market and in the surrounding streets is filled with lorries, vans and trolleys. The fire, by its very nature, could hardly be invisible, but between 10 p.m. and 4 a.m. it is peripheral to market activities and carries on without interference from anyone but the police. But from 4.30 a.m. until mid-day market activity renders the fire too exposed a place for dossers to frequent for long. Periodically market workers may burn some rubbish there and a dosser or two may come along, but this is no longer the dossers' fire. In talking of the fire, then, I have in mind the hours from about 10 p.m. to 4.30 a.m.

In contrast to the market, the fire attracts a cross-section of skid-row men. The dossers with whom this study is concerned are a part of, and in certain respects submerged in the wider skid-row population who gather around the fire nightly. I have already mentioned that dossers who are looking for work at the market tend to dismiss the men who stand around the fire as a bunch of jake-drinkers. Quite a bit of time is spent watching what is going on at the fire, or discussing the behaviour of its habitués. From the perspective of the dossers at the market entrance, there is an explicit polarity between the men at the market and those at the fire, which finds expression in the contrast between dosser and jake-drinker. However, from the viewpoint of those at the fire the picture looks different and is rather more complex.

"We're all dossers here" is a motif, constantly expressed, which shapes behaviour around the fire, and indicates that there is some pressure to play down potential divisions. The word "dosser" unites under one identity everyone at the fire. Their common perception of the way the police act, and what

they take to be police attitudes towards them, are significant factors, influencing both their attitudes towards each other and their response to the
police. The harassment by the police of the dossers at the fire—ordering them
to put out the fire, questioning them and dispersing them—demonstrates to
the latter that they occupy the same position in the eyes of the police.
Consequently, the social distinctions which receive such emphasis at other
times are put to one side in this context.

Nevertheless, although sentiments of "we're all dossers here" are real
enough, and find reinforcement as a result of the attentions of the police,
countervailing tendencies are evident. Indeed, the repeated assertion of
"we're all dossers here" suggests that the disharmony which comes from
emphasising divisions is always close at hand, and must be kept at bay by
stressing sentiments of unity if the different strands of the skid-row population
at the fire are to coexist. When social distinctions are brought to the surface
the category of jake-drinker is imposed by the men whom I studied on those
from whom they wish to separate themselves; the fire ceases to be simply a
dossers' locale and is redefined as a place used by two types of people:
dossers, that is those who are like oneself, and jake-drinkers, who are
different. From the point of view of the dossers, the fire becomes a different
place after the soup-run has departed. They come to the fire to pass an hour
or two in the earlier part of the night before the soup arrives, and then they
move off to their skippers or elsewhere. The fire, for them, is a gathering
point. The men who remain at the fire after the soup-run has departed are
regarded as jake-drinkers. To pass the greater part of the night by the fire
using it as a place to sleep, is interpreted by the dossers who are the subjects
of this article as the most evident destitution, and they strenuously repudiate
any common identity with these men. After all, the argument goes, dossers
know how to look after themselves, but if someone is reduced to sleeping by
the fire he has clearly let himself go.*

By contrast with the market entrance, where behaviour has continually to
be justified as appropriate, behaviour around the fire demands no such
justification, other than recognition that conflict should be suppressed because
"we're all dossers here". In practice this is a rather forlorn hope with frequent
arguments and provocation endemic to social intercourse at the fire. Half-
hearted attempts are sometimes made to keep the fire from becoming too
large, thereby attracting the attention of the police, and for the same reason
there is an occasional effort to silence men who are making a lot of noise.

---

* One would expect the men who pass the latter half of the night around the fire to contest
this viewpoint, and to provide their own interpretation of the situation. I say this partly
because all dossers justify their own behaviour in some manner, but more because of what
I reported in the footnote on p. 33, namely, the evidence we have already of significant differences in outlook and behaviour within skid row.

But in general it may be said that ideas of appropriate behaviour, which are strong at the market entrance and in skippers, are largely inapplicable at the fire. Significantly, when the police come to the fire nobody is blamed. This is probably because visits by the police are such a regular occurrence that it would be fruitless to find a scapegoat on each occasion. All the same, this lack of concern with apportioning blame at the fire, stands in marked contrast to the aftermath of police intervention in skippers.

While the contrast between the market entrance and the fire is an important one to the dossers at the market, such a contrast has no special significance for the dossers at the fire. They tend to recognise no difference of identity between those who frequent the two settings, and point out that the dossers who work at the market also pass time at the fire. In both milieux the distinction between dosser and jake-drinker serves to organise behaviour towards their fellows on skid row; the difference lies in where the boundary separating the two categories is to be drawn, and dossers who pass to and fro adopt the way of conceiving the distinction which is appropriate to the situation they are in.

Skippers

For most of us the question of where to sleep rarely occurs; it is an aspect of our lives which we take for granted, but for dossers it is a problematic area of their lives and a constant preoccupation. Many are faced each night with the question of where they are going to sleep, and although some find places which offer a degree of security, it is not surprising that discussion about places to sleep is a regular feature of their conversations. A fundamental distinction is drawn between staying in one of the formal institutions which cater for skid-row clientele, and "skippering". The institutions which dossers use include Salvation Army hostels, common-lodging houses, one or two commercial establishments, and also the government reception centre, the only one of these institutions for which dossers do not have to pay. The main characteristics of a skipper are that it is not an institution and does not cost any money. Skippers are places which dossers adapt to their own needs for shelter, and where they can avoid overt control by outsiders requiring conformity to a regime which is not of their own making. When dossers talk of "doing a skipper" or "skippering" they may use the term to denote an almost infinite array of places where it is possible to sleep, including places such as telephone kiosks, bus shelters or railway carriages. But more specifically a skipper is an empty or derelict building which provides scope for use over a longer period than the odd night or two. Many skippers, the more desirable ones, continue for a period of weeks or even months.

In assessing skippers as good or bad a number of considerations are brought into play. If a skipper is to survive for any length of time it is crucial that its existence is concealed. In the last resort this means that the police must remain in ignorance of the site having been turned into a skipper; for while it is acknowledged that they occasionally let a skipper continue because it is convenient for them to know where they can keep an eye on a number of dossers, from the dossers' point of view there can be neither privacy nor security in the knowledge that the police could visit at any time and have the place closed whenever they wish. To make sure that the police do not discover the whereabouts of a particular skipper it must also be concealed from the public. This entails that it should not be in such a busy or exposed setting that it is impossible to enter or leave it without being seen. Dossers profess to take great care in the way they enter and leave skippers in order to avoid attracting attention, doing so at times of day or night when there are few people around who might report them to the police. Lastly, other dossers must be kept unaware of its existence, for it is believed, the more who know about a skipper and attempt to use it themselves, the sooner it will come to the notice of the police. Secondary considerations in the dossers' valuation of a skipper include its physical condition, the facilities which it offers, and its convenience for other of the dossers' activities.

Nearly all dossers skipper from time to time, so how do they look on their companions in a skipper? In this context there are interesting contrasts with behaviour at the fire. So long as there is no trouble in the skipper which might lead to the police intervening and the local authority boarding up the building, dossers on the whole do not differentiate between themselves. At the same time, the greater the number of dossers using a particular skipper the more suspicious of each other they become, for a site becomes naturally increasingly hard to conceal when used by any number of people. Once trouble occurs, however, and inevitably when the police intervene, the precarious common identity of the participants is undermined, and the troublemakers are redefined as jake-drinkers. All the stereotypes which the dossers hold about jake-drinkers appear when a skipper breaks down: jake-drinkers are said to be rowdy, drinking noisily in groups in a way that is bound to attract attention; they are believed to be responsible for starting fires in skippers; their personal habits are revolting; and they are considered to lead such chaotic lives that they are unable to keep a skipper concealed. In a word, when a skipper fails, the category of "jake-drinker" offers a ready-made cause for the misfortune, and a term with discrediting connotations is imposed on those who are made the scapegoats.

Although dossers stress the necessity of concealing the whereabouts of good skippers, discretion is in fact rare. Above all, they say, it is vital that jake-drinkers should not get to hear of any viable skipper, for that would be the end of it within a day or two. But, as should be clear by now, jake-drinkers are not an identifiable group within the wider skid-row demain, in spite of the fact dossers use the term as if they were. Jake-drinkers arise out of redefining a social situation: men who are dossers in one context are derided as jake-drinkers in another. Consequently, despite insisting that information about skippers be guarded from jake-drinkers, it forms a staple of conversation at the fire as well as at the market entrance. Information about the locations of possible skippers is passed along the dossers' grape-vine, and a newcomer to the Spitalfields area could soon learn where to find a reasonable skipper.

Background Assumptions about the World

The behaviour of dossers in these various situations is more readily understood when it is placed in the context of certain general assumptions which they hold about their own lives. These assumptions are never invoked in the day-to-day justification of one's own actions and condemnation of the actions of others, which is carried on in virtually all situations. Indeed it is for this reason that I talk of "assumptions" for it is in the nature of an assumption that it is rarely made explicit. Although these assumptions must to some extent be inferred, they derive directly from the dosser's experience in the world, and at the same time provide him with a way of placing his everyday actions within the framework of a general rationale. The following assumptions strike me as important: the present is all that matters in dossers' lives; dossers are both free men and victims; dossers are alone in the world.

The present is all that matters in dossers' lives. In their daily lives at Spitalfields a temporal perspective is not a dimension which dossers call upon in their efforts to interpret and order the world. From the knowledge they carry of their former lives before they ended up as dossers, and from their contacts with various agencies of social control, they know that people in society at large are situated in social and personal terms by reference to their pasts and their future potential, but it does not feature in their daily interaction with each other. How a man came to be a dosser, and what his chances are of escaping skid row, may be burning questions for the professionals, but for the dossers themselves they are simply irrelevant considerations that cannot even be posed in terms of the day-to-day ideology of men in skid row.

There is some recognition of the past, chiefly exemplified in the wealth of stories which they tell about past incidents, some of which serve as a basis for the reputations of individual dossers. But this has no impact on the organisation of dossers' daily lives which are grounded in the present to an unusual degree. For the most part, dossers carry no social or personal definition of themselves or others based on the past, nor are expectations invested in the future. Social categorisation is freed largely from determination by the constraints of the past, and becomes a flexible process relating solely to the situation at hand as it is defined by the participants. Thus dossers act for short-term advantages, not as a matter of conscious intent, but because the actions of one day bear no implications for the actions of another day, and the vagaries of skid-row life discourage a man from looking ahead. Where social identities are manipulated for the purpose of projecting a superior status a dosser cannot carve out for himself an enduring status, but for the most part only advantages which are limited to the situation at hand. Furthermore, where past experience plays little or no part in the definition of the present, the notion of two actions being contradictory is quite inappropriate; behaviour is justified in any manner possible, without regard for the consistency with previous behaviour, which would be an irrelevant consideration.

Dossers are both free men and victims. Underlying many of the dossers' attitudes is an ambivalent conception of themselves, according to which they see themselves alternately as free men and as victims. Here I want to explore the ramifications of this ambivalence. On the rare occasions when dossers express a sense of freedom, they tend to emphasise their liberation from the "rat-race" and the concomitant obligations, expectations and demands which come with occupying a position in the wider society. This can be understood as the freedom of people who have nothing more to lose, but it is also a corollary of dossers' orientation to the present. By this I mean that a dosser is free in his interaction with other dossers because nothing he does is interpreted in the light of the past, nor does it convey any implications for the future. In other words, his sense of freedom is secured by the fact that he lives completely in the present.

This fact has important consequences, for when the dosser is confronted by a world in which people are defined primarily by reference to their past lives, then his conception of himself as a free man, dependent as it is to a considerable extent on his present-time perspective, becomes harder to sustain. This is precisely what happens when dossers encounter the agencies of social control, and it is these situations which nourish the dosser's view of himself as a victim.

A dosser's perception of himself as a victim, trapped in a world he cannot escape, operates on a number of different levels. His freedom is restricted because he receives continuous attention from the police, and he has to devote much of his time to making himself as invisible as possible. But more important than the fact of continuous police attention is the strongly held belief that society, in the shape primarily of police and courts, victimises the dosser for what he is, rather than dealing with him for what he does. The dosser can never gain acceptance for his definition of a situation in encounters with agents of social control, because there is what Becker (1967) has called a hierarchy of credibility which leads to discrimination between different perceptions of reality, making that of people such as dossers among the least acceptable. One fundamental aspect of the definition of reality which the dosser is forced to accept in these situations is a definition of himself based on past experience and future prognosis. In other words he is forced to recognise a conception of himself which is foreign to him in his daily interaction in the dosser's world. In encounters with agents of social control the dosser can sometimes manipulate situations to facilitate his own survival, but such strategies are constrained by the fact that he has lost the freedom to define himself and must do what he can with an unfamiliar self-image. Moreover, it is not simply through being forced to adopt an alien image of himself that he is stripped of the idea that he is a free man. For the picture of himself with which he is presented effectively disposes of the notion of the dosser as a free agent, untrammelled by the constraints which encumber the rest of society. When he perceives himself in the light of the past experiences which have brought him to skid row, and when he surveys the future possibilities which his predicament offers, a conception of himself as a victim or a prisoner—of his own behaviour, the behaviour of others, and of factors beyond his control—is inescapable. The limitations of the notion of the dosser as a free man are then manifest to him: namely those areas of the dosser's world which are relatively protected from outsiders; or to put the same thing in a different way, those situations in which the dosser can sustain a life orientated to the present.

Dossers are alone in the world. Dossers regard themselves as alone in the world, not in the sense that they do not mix with each other, but insofar as their social relations are marked by the minimum of obligations and ties. Sykes (1969a, b) in his description of a navvies' camp in Northern Scotland, noted a similar pattern of social relations based on the minimum of social ties and the rejection of mutual support. This assumption is closely related to the previous two. If the past signifies nothing for the present, then all past situations which might be used to construct a network of mutual rights and obligations will count for nothing.

There is no means to accumulate debits and credits in social relationships over a period of time, and while such an approach to living may foster a dosser's vision of himself as a free man, it also indicates his isolation. Dossers are doubly isolated. In the first place they are separated from the society into which they were born, and secondly the way they live isolates them effectively from others like themselves. Not only do they generally reject ties of mutual support, but additionally they rarely share a common perception of events, unless external pressure such as police harassment unites them temporarily.

Conclusion

The tacit assumptions which have just been discussed hold the key, I suggest, to an understanding of dossers' behaviour and their relationship to the wider society, for these form the basis of the dosser's ideology. The most striking feature of this ideology is the extent it institutionalises isolation from others who share the same environment and the same social identity. Reciprocity, by any definition one of the characteristics of a society, is rejected in theory, even though in practice it exists in the limited sphere of the exchange of information. There is admittedly a degree of cultural support which derives from a shared identity, shared life-style and shared habitat, but this cultural support rests not on ties of social solidarity, for these are repudiated at least at the conscious level, so much as on the fact that in an area frequented by others like himself a dosser can more easily hide anonymously. Furthermore, the dosser's perspective does its best to cut out the past and future as a frame of reference, and the dire consequences which ensue when dossers are forced to recognise a conception of themselves incorporating a temporal dimension have already been shown.

In this article I have described the ways in which one section of a skid-row population define themselves; my focus has been upon their own construction of reality. An inside view of the way people experience their lives makes it possible to correct to some extent assumptions imposed from outside—a necessary exercise when one is concerned with people such as dossers who are stigmatised as deviant, and whose own viewpoints receive scant respect in the wider society. However, while the intention has been to demonstrate the purposeful way in which dossers organise certain aspects of their lives on skid row, it would be misleading to ignore the external factors which impinge on and shape dossers' lives, all the more so when these influences are amply reflected in the ways dossers conceive of their experience.

One way of looking at a culture is to regard it as consisting of the rules, knowledge and attitudes which members of a society must learn if they are to operate in that society in a manner acceptable to their fellows (Goodenough, 1957). This perspective sheds an interesting light on the way of life of dossers, for it enables us to delineate clearly the constituents of the specifically skid-row culture. What dossers have to learn in order to function as dossers may be summed up as follows:

(i) The unstated principles, or tacit assumptions which I have just described.

(ii) A scheme of social classification, the crux of which consists of the elaboration of a dichotomy between dossers, an acceptable identity, and jake-drinkers, a label with pejorative connotations and an identity which, while it may be acceptable to certain skid-row men, would be rejected by the men who are the subjects of this article as a fitting description of themselves, although each of them would be happy to impose it on others from whom they wished to distinguish themselves.

(iii) A variety of distinctive terms for relevant aspects of their lives. These might be described as the dosser's argot, yet against that such terms are few, and they resemble rather the semi-specialised or colloquial usages of workers in a particular field.

(iv) Knowledge of a range of strategies for making out in the world. These are very often of considerable complexity, and revolve around three paramount concerns: how to obtain money, how to find shelter, and how to evade the attentions of the police.

Viewed in this light the extent of these aspects of the dosser's culture which is unique to skid row are manifested. Many basic concepts and categories remain those of the social world in which they grew up but from which they are now separated. Separation, indeed, imbues the dosser's culture. In the underlying assumptions which guide their behaviour, and in the strategies which dossers learn in order to survive, we are presented with a separation which is two-fold. Dossers are cut-off from the social world in which they formerly had membership, although they retain to a large extent the cultural perspective of this world. But equally dossers live in a state of separation from each other, avoiding commitments with their fellows as assiduously as they avoid constraints imposed on them by external agencies. The restricted development of the dossers' own cultural forms is due partly to the fact that nobody is born a dosser, but another factor which must be taken into account is the isolationist tenor of their lives among themselves, the lack of reciprocity which I have already mentioned. A way of life which puts strict limits on any mutuality and institutionalises isolation between individuals who lead this life effectively restricts the cultural resources which will be created.

One key question emerges from this study. Research in this country (Archard, 1976) and in the United States (Wiseman, 1970) has shown that the social organisation of skid-row alcoholics incorporates a much greater degree of mutual support, social solidarity and reciprocity than was in evidence among the dossers with whom I have been concerned in this article, who appear to have more in common with the navvies described by Sykes (1969a, b). Why this should be the case, and indeed whether, as seems likely, there are more complex variations in the forms of social organisation of different sectors of the skid-row population, is a topic for further exploration.

References

Archard, P. (1975). "The Bottle won't Leave You: A Study of Homeless Alcoholics and their Guardians." Alcoholics Recovery Project, London.

P. Phillimore

Becker, H. (1967). Whose side are we on? *Soc. Prob.* **14**, 239–247.
Goodenough, W. H. (1957). "Cultural Anthropology and Linguistics" (Garvin, P. L., ed.) Report of the Seventh Annual Round Table Meeting on Linguistics and Language Study, Georgetown University Monograph Series on Language and Linguistics.
Orwell, G. (1966). "Down and Out in Paris and London." Penguin, Harmondsworth.
Sykes, A. J. (1969a). Navvies. Their work attitudes. *Sociology,* **3**, 21–35.
Sykes, A. J. (1969b). Navvies. Their social relations. *Sociology*, **3**, 157–172.
Wiseman, J. P. (1970). "Stations of the Lost: The treatment of the Skid Row Alcoholic." Prentice-Hall, New Jersey.

The Evaluation of a Voluntary Organisation Attempting to Resettle Destitute Men: Action Research with the St. Mungo Community Trust

JOHN LEACH

Introduction

The St. Mungo Community Trust is a London-based voluntary organisation concerned with the welfare and resettlement of destitute men. In September 1971, it received a grant from the Department of Health and Social Security, guaranteeing a degree of support for several years, and providing a small research team from the Institute of Psychiatry, London University, in order to evaluate the effectiveness of its services. The team adopted an action research approach. On the completion of an initial phase of evaluation, tentative conclusions were drawn and communicated to the management and staff of the Community, who then had the option of altering their procedures. Another phase of evaluation, with the same aim as before, was then undertaken by the research team. Thus the research proceeded in cycles of evaluation, policy change, re-evaluation, and further policy change.

The present chapter describes the progress of the action research, and discusses the implications of its outcome. The chapter contains four parts: a summary of the aims and methods of St. Mungo's at the time the action research began, in January 1972; a description of the stages of action research and details of the techniques used to measure the effectiveness of St. Mungo's; an account of the findings of the evaluation of effectiveness;

and a discussion of the implications of these findings for the provision of services for destitute men.

The Aims and Policies of the St. Mungo Community Trust

The St. Mungo Community Trust was founded in London in May 1969, by an ex-worker of the Simon Community. The main aim of St. Mungo's was to help men who had no material possessions or resources and who slept rough, to find and maintain acceptable independent accommodation in the community. This aim of resettlement was not fundamentally different from that of reception centres; the methods used by St. Mungo's however, were different to those of statutory agencies.*

St. Mungo's made contact with men on the streets by means of a soup-run which operated every night of the year in the West End of London. As well as providing food the soup-run enabled St. Mungo's to make regular contact with men sleeping out. The St. Mungo staff (called workers) were young volunteers who worked on the soup-run and in Community houses for a year or so in return for a token payment. The workers believed that giving out soup regularly and unconditionally would make it possible for some destitute men to respond to them as ordinary people rather than as social workers, and that, in this way, mutual relationships of trust and confidence could develop between them and the men. It was intended that the relationships built up between workers and men on the soup-run should be developed and deepened in the more intimate atmosphere of the St. Mungo houses.

St. Mungo's provided short-lease terraced houses as accommodation for the men brought back from the soup-run. The houses were capable of accommodating 10–15 residents and two or three workers. The characteristics of these houses—small environments where a good deal of social contact (e.g. in the kitchen) could not be avoided—were thought by the workers to present many opportunities for close social interaction between themselves

---

* Reception centres are the modern equivalents of the workhouses and casual wards that were established in Britain during the nineteenth century. They are government establish-ments administered by the Supplementary Benefits Commission for the Department of Health and Social Security. The responsibilities of reception centres are laid down in the Ministry of Social Security Act 1966 and formerly in the National Assistance Act 1948. Schedule 4, section 2(1) of the more recent Act describes the duty "to make provision whereby persons without a settled way of living may be influenced to lead a more settled life" and to "provide and maintain centres to be known as reception centres for the provision of temporary board and lodging for such persons." "Persons without a settled way of living" is the modern euphemism for the old terms, "tramps", "vagrants", and "wayfarers".

and the men. The houses were usually rather shabby and untidy since the workers believed that worn, and even uncomfortable, surroundings would be most acceptable to men coming straight from the streets. This view was based on the belief that an uncomfortable environment would be easier to adjust to for men who had been living rough. The same belief led to an attempt to construct a tier system within groups of houses, in which some houses were made more comfortable than others. It was thought by the workers that a developing ability of men to maintain themselves in independent accommodation should be encouraged by providing, at different stages of their residence in the Community, houses of an increasing standard of comfort.

Until the spring of 1975, St. Mungo's operated a "no-drink rule", and residents who drank alcohol (whether on or off St. Mungo premises) were liable to be asked to leave the Community. The St. Mungo management said that this rule had been introduced, at the request of residents, shortly after the founding of St. Mungo's.

Within the houses the workers performed several roles. They adopted, if requested, the role of intermediary between residents and various kinds of official authority. In this capacity they attempted to deal with many of the problems that a resident encountered, such as complications over Social Security benefits and hospital appointments.

In some houses the workers did all the cooking; whether this occurred depended on the inclinations of residents in particular houses, since all residents were free to help, or not help, as they wished. The houses were run informally by the workers, who attempted to avoid, as far as was possible, any behaviour that could be interpreted by the residents as being censorious or authoritarian. The workers intended that the relatively permissive atmosphere of the houses should provide a bridge between the life-style of men who slept rough and the restrictions of everyday social life. When the research began a "three day" rule was operated by St. Mungo's. The majority of men admitted to houses were allowed three days' residence before referral to an outside agency. In practice, however, this time period was often extended.

Initially, the Community consisted of only one house in south London which was let by Wandsworth Council at a nominal rent. From May 1970, however, St. Mungo's began to expand, acquiring several other houses on short lease. The DHSS grant, awarded to St. Mungo's in September 1971, enabled this expansion to continue, and in January 1972 when the research began, St. Mungo's possessed four residential houses, accommodating between them, forty to fifty men.*

---

* No women were admitted to St. Mungo houses during the research period. It was St. Mungo policy to refer destitute women met on the soup-run to agencies specifically established to accommodate women. The St. Mungo management felt that these agencies could better meet the women's needs.

Criteria of Effectiveness and the Stages of Action Research

Introduction

It has been suggested that the major problem for evaluation studies is that of defining the aims of the agency under investigation, since the purpose of evaluation is to provide "objective, systematic and comprehensive evidence of the degree to which the program achieves its intended objectives" (Hyam *et al.*, 1962). The difficulty about accepting this suggestion at its face value is two-fold. In the first place, the agency may not have unambiguous, or even generally agreed, aims. In the second place, the research team may discern covert aims in the practice of the agency, which are at variance with its public statements (Leach and Wing, 1978).

For these reasons it has been suggested that any evaluative research must test not only the overt aims of the agency but also any aims that seem implicit in its organisation and practice (Wing, 1973). This principle is particularly important in action research, since one of its most useful consequences may be to help the agency redefine its objectives.

The St. Mungo action research project proceeded in stages (Leach and Wing, in press). At intervals throughout the project, recommendations were made to the St. Mungo management which, if accepted, were subsequently evaluated. This research approach was adopted because the research team believed, following Marris and Rein (1967), that it is easier to make rational policy choices if a plan of action is broken down into a series of proximate steps. The approach attempts to reduce the unknown factors relevant to decisions by concentrating on the short time period between each step.

The St. Mungo research team therefore presented its recommendations in discrete packages, each separated by a period of time during which action could be evaluated. It was not, of course, assumed at the outset of the project that progress could be as rational as this model suggests. The administration of any complex service presents problems that require decision without undue delay, and the research team accepted that it must try to catch up with such changes as they occurred. In fact the various stages of action were fairly clear-cut. There were eight distinct points at which research findings were translated into recommendations for action. The main research recommendations (of which the first was the most important for the action research project and provided the focus for much of the rest of the research) were as follows:

(i) addition of the goal of settlement in sheltered accommodation to that of resettlement in an independent mode of living,

(ii) provision of a night shelter,

(iii) adoption of a daytime programme in order to supplement the contacts made with destitute men on the nightly soup-run,

(iv) appointment of skilled group leaders (in charge of a group of houses) and a skilled person to supervise the soup-run, in order to guide the work of enthusiastic but untrained volunteers,

(v) early readmission of men who left houses,

(vi) modification of the "no drink" rule,

(vii) involvement of house workers in the assessment of residents' needs and the formulation of a programme of help for each resident,

(viii) institution of a routine assessment of men referred to houses from the night-shelter.

A number of developments occurred in St. Mungo's that did not arise out of specific recommendations by the research team, and these will be described in due order.

Pilot Survey

The chief aim of St. Mungo's was to help destitute men settle in suitable independent accommodation; at best paying their own way, but otherwise with the aid of Social Security payments. The early pamphlets and reports of the Community claimed a good deal of success in this direction, stating that St. Mungo's was successful in partially or fully rehabilitating about 70% of the men with whom it came into contact. However, the first enquiries of the research team (which took the form of participant observation, on the soup-run and in the houses) suggested that the aim of resettlement in independent accommodation was not often fulfilled. The pilot phase of research was designed both to throw light on this fundamental question and to describe the characteristics of the men admitted to St. Mungo houses, in order to better define their needs. At the same time, the research team formulated a more restricted aim for the Trust, based on its own observations. It was our view that St. Mungo's should try to help destitute men to stay in its houses long enough for any rehabilitation procedures it offered to have an influence. If this basic aim was not being achieved, the resettlement of men in independent accommodation seemed unlikely.

The pilot study therefore had two aims. The first aim was to discover whether either the general objective of St. Mungo's, or the more restricted objective formulated for the Community by the research team, was being achieved. This could be investigated by means of a follow-up study, which would enquire into the residence of men after discharge, and by recording how long men stayed in the houses. The second aim was to describe the characteristics and attitudes of the men.

There seemed no point, at this stage, in mounting a controlled or compara-

c

tive trial, since the objectives of St. Mungo's had to be clarified first. Only if the rate of resettlement was shown to be fairly high would it be worth considering more elaborate evaluative designs, in order to discover whether St. Mungo's was more effective than other voluntary or statutory agencies.

The pilot study was carried out during the first three months of 1972. The 35 men in residence in the four St. Mungo houses (comprising an assessment centre and three associated houses) on 1 January 1972, and the 70 men admitted to these houses during the following three months, formed the sample. A check on the whereabouts of men resident in the houses at the beginning of January, or admitted during February, was made during the first week of April. A minimum of two months was therefore allowed for the follow-up. It was assumed by the research team that any placement made, and held, during the first few weeks after discharge, would be crucial to subsequent outcome.

Characteristics of the Men Admitted

The men's characteristics were not greatly different from those found in the earlier studies of destitute men, summarised by Tidmarsh and Wood (1972). Two-thirds of the men admitted to St. Mungo houses were aged over 40, and two-thirds came from the north of England, Ireland or Scotland. Over half were single and only 7 % were still married. Two-thirds had had no recent contact with family members. The precarious economic situation of these men was apparent from their occupational histories and from the kinds of accommodation they had recently lived in. Three-quarters of the men had worked mainly in unskilled manual work, although two-thirds had had some kind of work during the year prior to their admission to St. Mungo's, even if only briefly. Nearly a third of the men said they had spent most of the year prior to their admission sleeping rough, and most of the rest had stayed in reception centres, lodging-houses, hostels, hospitals or prisons during this period. Only 13 % had been living in their own accommodation, in private lodgings, or with relatives. About half the men mentioned a prison sentence during the year before their admission to a house.

A psychiatrist was able to interview 67 of the men. Only one man was suffering from schizophrenia. Depression was more common but it was only severe in one out of six diagnosed cases. Severe alcoholism was present in eight cases. One man was regarded as mentally retarded and two suffered from epilepsy. The incidence of mental disability among this group was therefore lower than that found in some other surveys of destitute men (Lodge-Patch, 1970; Priest, 1970). Serious physical illness among these men was, however, quite common; one-third had a serious physical illness during the year prior to their admission, usually respiratory. Varicose veins, ankle oedema, and suchlike "conditions of vagrancy" were also common.

Those men who stayed in the St. Mungo houses for more than three months had rather different characteristics from those who left earlier. The "longer-stay" men were older, more likely to have been born in England or Wales, but were less likely to have had a problem with alcohol or to have been to prison. All the men with severe psychiatric conditions stayed for more than three months.

The men using St. Mungo's possessed, therefore, similar characteristics to the destitute men interviewed by other investigators. They were usually middle-aged or old, tended to come from Scotland, Ireland or the north of England, and had little contact with their relatives. Most of the men had a long experience of sleeping rough and living in lodging-houses or reception centres, and many had experience of other institutions such as prisons and psychiatric hospitals.

Findings of the Follow-up Enquiry

Of the 64 men who were resident in St. Mungo houses on 1 January 1972 (N=35), or who were admitted to houses during February (N=29), only eight were untraced by the research team during the first week of May. Most of the untraced men had only stayed a day or two in the houses and were thought (on the basis of the outcome of previous admissions) to have returned to their former way of life. Ten men had left St. Mungo's to live with relatives or friends, or had succeeded in finding lodgings or their own room, or Part III accommodation.* It is doubtful, however, whether more than three of these men could be said to have changed from a completely rootless way of life to something more settled, as a result of spending several months in St. Mungo houses.

Of the remaining 46 men whose whereabouts were known, five were in prison at the time of follow-up, 14 were living rough (all these men were in touch with the soup-run), and 27 were still resident in St. Mungo houses. The main characteristic of the St. Mungo houses, therefore, was a rapid turnover of residents, with two-thirds of the men admitted to houses being back on the streets within a week of their admission. About 15% of the men admitted to houses stayed for three months or more. Three men who left after a prolonged stay in a St. Mungo house (5% of the men followed-up) seemed to have been helped to a stable resettlement.

These findings resulted in the first research recommendations of the action research project.

---

* Part III of the National Assistance Act 1948, left local authorities with the duty of providing for those who needed residential accommodation. The growing number of old people has meant that the major part of these responsibilities have concerned care for the aged.

The First Four Research Recommendations

The pilot study described above indicated that a large proportion of the men admitted to St. Mungo houses not only had a long history of social disadvantage, but were handicapped by physical or psychiatric disabilities or alcoholism. The follow-up study showed that most of these men stayed only a very brief time in the houses and then returned to the sort of life they had been living before.

The research team suggested, on the basis of these findings, that the central functions of St. Mungo's were two-fold. In the first place there was the humanitarian function of supplying food and shelter to people who lacked them. This should be continued, the more so since it allowed the second function to be carried out. This function was one of resettlement, not only in the sense of helping some destitute men to secure independent accommodation, but also (and we considered this the more sizeable role of St. Mungo's), to give these men an opportunity to settle, if they wished, in the St. Mungo houses. A policy of resettlement of this kind would necessitate an increase in the medium and longer-term accommodation provided by St. Mungo's and would entail a lesser emphasis on the rapid turnover of men in the houses.

This recommendation was accepted by the St. Mungo management which took steps to facilitate the working of the new policy of resettlement. A second group of houses was added to the Community, and a third group of houses (originally created to help house men made homeless when Butterwick Rowton House, a lodging house in West London, was closed by the local authority) was also integrated into the St. Mungo system. The number of men accommodated in St. Mungo houses increased from an average of 42 per night at the beginning of the research project to an average of 84 at its end. The expectation on the part of St. Mungo staff, that men would rapidly move on, was changed and the staff encouraged men to stay for longer periods. The implication of this policy change was that longer-term houses would have to be set up, and bed-sitter accommodation provided for those men who could achieve a degree of independence. In this way it would be possible to provide a structure in which men could move from the streets to a position of relative independence.

A further implication of the new policy was that other arrangements would have to be made for the men who had previously been admitted to St. Mungo houses for only a few nights and who had then returned to the streets. The research team thought that the emphasis placed by the Community on the soup-run was correct, since it fostered contact with men on the streets (many of the men contacted during the follow-up enquiry were met on the soup-run) and allowed an opportunity for St. Mungo workers to assess the men's needs and attitudes. Because of the informal nature of work on the soup-run, however, it was easy for workers to lose the value of initial contacts, especially since many of them only went out on the soup-run once a week. It seemed sensible therefore to have a soup-run director who could receive reports on any promising contacts made by workers, and ensure that they were followed up. This particular recommendation was not accepted by the St. Mungo management and the importance given to the soup-run by the management gradually declined (see p. 62).

However, the second major recommendation of the research team, that a night shelter should be established in order to foster contact with men who stayed for only a night or two in the St. Mungo houses, was accepted. At the end of March 1973, a night shelter, catering for 50 men, was opened in a disused church, St. Anne's in Westminster, central London. By mid-October 1973, there were five full-time workers at the night shelter, together with a variable number of inexperienced volunteers who worked there in a probationary capacity. Men were admitted to the shelter, by ticket but without charge, after 8 p.m., and had to leave by 7 a.m. the following morning (8 a.m. on Sundays). Whilst staying at the shelter the men were given soup, bread and tea and a breakfast of porridge. In December 1973, this shelter was supplemented by a much larger building, an old Marmite factory in the south London district of Vauxhall. The Marmite shelter could accommodate as many as 200 people. In the spring of 1975 the St. Anne's shelter was closed and night shelter was provided only in the Marmite building.

The third recommendation of the research team was that the soup-run and night shelter should be supplemented by efforts on the part of St. Mungo's to contact destitute men during the daytime. A campaign known as "Winter Survival" was started by St. Mungo's in November 1972, and this culminated in a three-day outdoor Christmas party for destitute men at the old Covent Garden Market in central London. During the campaign an ambulance was acquired by St. Mungo's and used to tour areas of likely day-time contact, in order to provide practical medical, personal and welfare help for the destitute men encountered. Those men who were ill when met on the streets, were taken to hospitals or G.P.s and a nurse working on the project provided immediate basic treatment for the men if this was necessary. Other men were met simply for a cup of tea and conversation. A further campaign of this kind was begun by St. Mungo's in October 1973, but the expense of these enterprises was considerable and they were ended when St. Mungo's became unable to afford the running costs of the ambulance.

During the period October 1972–April 1973, the research team made a study of the differences between men who left St. Mungo houses relatively quickly and men who stayed in houses three months or more. It was found that the attitudes of the two groups were different. Those men who left houses relatively quickly were less likely than the "longer-stay" men to feel that they needed help and were less likely to identify themselves with other destitute men who they tended to see as "different". Since these data suggested that there was a group of men who might have little motivation to accept the services that St. Mungo's offered, the research team recommended that day contact with this group should be intensified and that, to facilitate this contact, a day centre should be provided. We further suggested that, within part of the day centre, the "no drink" rule could be relaxed since this might encourage a wider group of men to visit the centre.

A day centre was not in fact set up. It would have been expensive and other projects were given priority by the St. Mungo management (see p. 62). Close ties between St. Mungo's and a separate day centre in central London were, however, established. Ideas for providing some form of remunerative "sheltered" work were approved by the St. Mungo management but could not be put into operation or, like a St. Mungo workshop set up in the west London district of Notting Hill in November 1972, proved to be economically unviable. The workshop had facilities for renovating furniture. The premises were small and only a few men were able to work there.

The fourth recommendation the research team made on the basis of the findings of the pilot survey was that skilled leaders should be appointed to each group of St. Mungo houses and that a further skilled worker should direct the soup-run. The word "skill" was defined in two ways. We felt that some members of the St. Mungo staff should have previous experience of working with destitute men and, if possible, should also possess professional training of a relevant kind. This recommendation reflected changes that were occurring in the St. Mungo Community. A St. Mungo pamphlet, issued after the pilot survey, discussed the changing role of the worker. After describing the "framework of near equality" between workers and residents that had previously existed in the St. Mungo houses, the pamphlet concluded that:

> whilst attempting to keep the principles of the Community with regard to equality firmly in mind, it has nevertheless been essential for the continuity and expansion of the project to provide adequate salaries to attract certain kinds of workers, especially senior workers, who would wish to spend some considerable period of time in the Community.

The document further stated that three senior social workers and a deputy director were ready to commence work and that an Administrator had been appointed.

Eventually group leaders were appointed to take charge of all three groups of St. Mungo houses. They included people with relevant experience in social work, the probation service and the rehabilitation of prisoners. Workers with a long experience of the Community also worked in this capacity.

Early Readmission of Men after Leaving the Houses (Fifth Research Recommendation)

A statistical register of admissions and discharges of men using St. Mungo houses was established by the research team in October 1972, with a census of men resident on the first of the month. It was clear after a year or so that none of the measures so far adopted by the Community had resulted in men staying longer in the St. Mungo houses (the statistics relating to this are presented later). During the spring of 1974, the research team suggested that it might be fruitful (in order to capitalise on contacts already made between the workers and destitute men) to concentrate attention on the large group of men (two-thirds of all discharges) with whom St. Mungo workers kept in contact, usually by meeting them on the soup-run. We suggested to St. Mungo's that these men should, if they wished, be readmitted to houses as soon as possible after leaving.

This recommendation was accepted by the Community. It reflected an earlier Community policy which St. Mungo's had claimed was successful in persuading men to settle in its houses and which the research team wanted to evaluate. In a St. Mungo document entitled, "Report of the First Year's Work" (1970), it was stated by the Community that:

> We have found that he [destitute man invited back to a house] who stays on his first try, never makes much progress. He inevitably shows promise and mixes well, but he cannot seem to stand the strain of total acceptance and thus departs, usually after about ten days. We have found that [there is a] magic figure of fourth time lucky [i.e. on his fourth stay in a house the man would remain]. During his periods of coming and going, [the destitute man] is obviously seeking our motive, he feels it is too good to be true, being a fatalist he is seeking the inevitable catch.

The emphasis here was on a cumulative effect. St. Mungo's postulated that destitute men, homeless in some cases for many years, could only gradually be induced to resettle. There was no evidence that this was so, since the variables affecting the process were only vaguely defined, and many men known to the research team had spent more than four periods in St. Mungo houses without showing any tendency to stay more than a few days there. However, it was possible that such a process might operate over a longer period of time. We therefore suggested that it would be worth giving special attention to men discharged after a brief stay. This recommendation was discussed at a St. Mungo conference held in May 1974, and it was agreed by the management that it should be implemented. The new system was quickly put into operation and was effective, in the sense that the statistical register recorded a concentration on men who had previously been admitted to St. Mungo houses. Unfortunately, however, the new policy did not result in the men admitted to houses staying any longer than before.

Modification of the "No Drink" Rule (Sixth Research Recommendation)

Due to the failure of the measures described above to help men settle in the St. Mungo houses, the research team decided to undertake an enquiry into the reasons why men were leaving the Community. The data obtained from the enquiry were used as a basis for further recommendations. Information was obtained about 64 men who left St. Mungo houses during October and November 1974, nearly half of whom were interviewed. Data on the reasons why the others had left were obtained from the men's case-notes and from St. Mungo workers. Eleven men had left houses because of difficulties with other residents (often one particular man who was found irritating). Such problems were often the result of intolerance of handicap in others. Three residents gave dislike of workers as their reason for leaving the houses; these men thought the house regime too rigid and censorious. Only one man gave dissatisfaction with amenities as a reason for leaving a house, but two men found their house dull and boring and two thought there was too high a turnover of men in their house with not enough stability. Only one man gave lack of contact with friends outside as his main reason for leaving.

About half the men had left the houses because they were determined to have a drink and could not do so while remaining in St. Mungo accommodation, or because they were asked to leave by staff when it was discovered that they had been drinking. Not all these men were "problem" drinkers in the sense that their drinking could not be controlled; about one-third seemed to be "social drinkers" whose drinking usually remained under control.

"Wilfred", for example, a social drinker, was asked to leave when he returned to a house after drinking a moderate amount. When asked his opinion of the "no-drink" rule he said:

> it is much too strict. If you have half a pint it has the same consequence as being drunk. This total ban on drinking makes relationships difficult. How are you supposed to explain to your friends at work that you can't go to the pub with them because you're not allowed to drink? I wouldn't mind other residents coming into the house if they'd had a drink or two. If they behaved badly, the rest of the residents would be quite capable of dealing with them. If we were allowed this responsibility we'd feel it was more our house.

"Wilfred" found the house satisfactory in other respects. It was "comfortable" and he had had no wish to leave it.

"Brian", by contrast, had an alcohol problem which he recognised as serious; he had specifically left the house to go drinking. He said:

> I felt that I had to have a drink, I left because I wouldn't break the rule by drinking in a house. I liked everything about the house when I was there.

It was magic after what I'd been used to. I really liked one of the house workers. We had known each other a long time on the soup-run before I was ever invited back to a house. The other residents in the house were fairly easy to get on with. Drinkers that I knew lived in St. Mungo houses a short distance away and we used to visit each other. One used to come over here for breakfast sometimes. As far as the drink is concerned it's the total abstinence that creates such strain. I know full well that I need to drink but I can do it in moderation if I have to. I've managed it when I've been working. They don't like you drunk there.

None of the men interviewed expressed a wish to go back to sleeping rough. Some, especially among the "social drinker" group, were bitter about the way they had been treated by St. Mungo's. A minority of men, at the time of interview, were uncertain whether they wanted anything more to do with the Community. Only one man who had left St. Mungo's because of drinking thought that the "no drink" rule, as it was then applied, was beneficial to residents.

On the basis of these findings the research team recommended that St. Mungo's relax the "no drink" rule for an experimental period. We also suggested that St. Mungo's should cease to treat drinkers as a homogeneous group and should plan its house facilities accordingly.

St. Mungo's accepted this recommendation and the "no drink" rule was relaxed for an experimental period beginning on 1st April 1975. The new policy stated that residents would only be refused entry to a house if they were actually drunk, or if their behaviour, whether they were drunk or not, seemed likely to upset other residents. Even if a man was drunk, he would be free to return to a house as soon as he had sobered up. Drinking in the houses was still forbidden. Weekly meetings were to be held at which group leaders, workers and a member of the research team would be present. These meetings would discuss the reactions of different residents to the new policy. If a resident continually returned to a house drunk, or if he persistently annoyed other men staying in the house whilst under the influence of drink, he would be asked to leave. This could not take place, however, until the next weekly meeting was convened and the decision had to be accepted by a majority of the St. Mungo staff present.

Although the new policy regarding drinking was generally welcomed by workers and men, and seemed to operate well in practice, in that fears of abuse of the new freedom were unfounded, it did not result in many men staying longer in houses than they had stayed before. Before describing the seventh and eighth recommendations that the research team made in an attempt to reverse this lack of success, an outline is given of events occurring in St. Mungo's that did not arise directly from research recommendations.

Further Changes in the St. Mungo Community 1974–1975

In May 1974, St. Mungo's acquired the former Charing Cross Hospital in central London, which had accommodation for nearly 200 men, mostly in 10 dormitories, but with a number of cubicles and single rooms. The Hospital was intended by St. Mungo's to offer accommodation of a lodging-house kind, primarily for working men.

In December 1974, a large bed-sitter complex, called Lennox Buildings, was opened by St. Mungo's in Vauxhall, South London. This accommodation comprised about 60 beds, mostly in single rooms, and was intended for men without severe disability or disturbance, since very little supervision was available. Most men who settled there were, in fact, referred from agencies other than St. Mungo's. In a census of Lennox residents taken on 1st October 1975, the research team found that only seven out of 56 Lennox residents were from St. Mungo houses. These developments did not therefore much affect the situation in the houses.

A decision that did, however, directly concern house workers, was that they should no longer operate the soup-run. From April 1975, the soup-run was run by inexperienced volunteers who found it difficult to get to know the men they contacted, partly because there was no senior worker available who knew many of these men well, and partly because the volunteers did not service the soup-run sufficiently regularly or often to build up such experience for themselves. This change was made by the St. Mungo management on the grounds that soup-run work, in addition to duties in the houses, was an excessive strain on workers. Few workers agreed with this view and most were critical of the change in policy. The new soup-run policy was not in line with the fourth recommendation of the research team which had suggested that the soup-run should be regularly serviced by a group of experienced workers.

The Involvement of Houseworkers in the Assessment of Men's Needs (Seventh Research Recommendation)

The research team's enquiry into the men's reasons for leaving described on p. 60, had indicated that a more systematic and detailed analysis of each resident's characteristics and needs would be useful. Three separate assessments of men who had stayed as long as a month in two groups of St. Mungo houses were made during 1975, in order to estimate the men's drinking and social behaviour. Consideration of this behaviour would suggest whether a specialised rather than a mixed house might be a more suitable environment for some of these men. The assessments were undertaken by a member of the research team in consultation with group leaders and workers. The aim of the exercise was to derive an appropriate "treatment" plan for each resident, and assess the likelihood of his eventual resettlement outside St. Mungo's.

Current behaviour in respect of alcohol (that is, behaviour exhibited during the man's present period of house residence) was classified as non-drinking, social or controlled drinking (an occasional episode of drunkenness was accepted), or uncontained drinking; the last category was reserved for frequent bouts of drinking usually leading to drunkenness. A few cases on the borderline between the second and third categories were placed into the second but, in general, the distinctions were not difficult to make.

Social behaviour was classified according to a hierarchy, with "aggression" at the top. Only a man who was quite often physically violent or very verbally abusive was regarded as aggressive. A second category of behaviour (not used unless the man was non-aggressive according to the above definition) was "eccentricity", applied only when a man's behaviour was decidedly odd or inexplicable. A man who frequently laughed and talked to himself, or who had very unusual mannerisms, or was extremely suspicious of everyone and everything without apparent reason, would be regarded as showing eccentric behaviour. There was no question of any diagnosis of illness; the observation was purely behavioural. A third category, only used if the other two were absent, was "withdrawal". Again, only very marked and active withdrawal was accepted for a positive rating.

On none of the three occasions of assessment was any man who had been in a St. Mungo house for longer than a month regarded as markedly aggressive. This finding reflected St. Mungo policy since men exhibiting very aggressive behaviour were usually asked to leave the houses. About one-third of the men were regarded as markedly eccentric (many of these men were also very withdrawn). About half of this group were known to have been in psychiatric hospitals and several more had clear-cut psychiatric symptoms at the time of assessment. These men tended to stay in the Community for the longest periods. Marked withdrawal, unassociated with eccentric behaviour, was not common among the house residents (only 7 % of the men). By far the largest group, approximately two-thirds of the men in the houses, consisted of residents who did not show any of these characteristics to a marked degree. While frequent uncontained drinking was not uncommon (18 % on average at the three assessments), 40 % of the men were able to take an occasional drink without getting drunk. The rest of the men did not drink at all.

An estimate of the optimum type of accommodation the men could hope to obtain, and of their need for care, was also made on these three occasions. These estimates were based on a judgment, made by the St. Mungo staff and one of the research team, about the ability of residents to look after themselves in various kinds of accommodation. This judgment was partly derived from an assessment of illness, handicap and infirmity. The resident's likely reaction to a move was also considered. For example, a man without serious medical impairments, whose social relationships were limited to the house, and who was known to have been solitary and destitute for a long period before entering St. Mungo's, would not necessarily be expected to move.

The options available to the men lay between remaining in a St. Mungo house for a long, medium or short period of time (defined respectively as one year plus, six months to a year, and under six months), transferring to a St. Mungo bed-sitter, the Charing Cross Hospital or Lennox Buildings, or moving into more independent accommodation such as a flat or private lodgings. These alternatives represented progressively lesser degrees of care. The assessments were distributed in much the same way on each of the three occasions. Most of the men were regarded as needing to stay for a long period of time in a St. Mungo house. This was particularly true of those men whose behaviour had been regarded as eccentric or withdrawn. Overall, 57% of the men were thought to need long-term, 18% medium-term, and 2% short-term care in St. Mungo houses; 16% were thought to need a St. Mungo bed-sitter and 7% other types of accommodation. There was little relationship between these accommodation plans and drinking behaviour.

However, in spite of these assessment exercises and a resulting increase in the understanding of the men's behaviour by St. Mungo workers, there was still no evidence that a larger number of men were settling in St. Mungo houses. The number of men admitted to houses had diminished towards the end of the year, because more men were considered unsuitable and were excluded, but the proportion of men who remained for long periods in the houses did not increase.

The Institution of a Routine Assessment of all Men Referred to St. Mungo Houses from the Night Shelter (Eighth Research Recommendation)

In order to utilise the experience and information derived from the assessment exercises and apply them directly to the admission process, a routine referral procedure was suggested by the research team and adopted by St. Mungo's in November 1975. Men staying in the Marmite night shelter (which now housed up to 150 men a night), who seemed possibly suitable for admission to a St. Mungo house, were discussed at a weekly meeting at which the Deputy Director, a Marmite worker, the Group 1 leader, representatives of workers in all three groups, and a member of the research team were present. The aim of the meeting was not only to assess whether an individual seemed likely to settle in a St. Mungo house, but also to consider which house would provide the most congenial atmosphere and company for him. Most admissions of men to houses were subsequently made after following this procedure.

It quickly became apparent that the new procedure for selecting men for

St. Mungo houses was successful in the sense that most men admitted to the houses tended to settle. This development was so pronounced that by August 1976, 60% of St. Mungo residents had been in houses for a year or more, and virtually all had been resident for more than three months. Interviews conducted by the research team in April 1976, showed that the men now accumulating had long histories of destitution and that at least half of them were severely handicapped. Psychiatric impairments were particularly prominent.* By the Summer of 1976, the movement of men through the St. Mungo houses had virtually stopped since the houses had no vacant places.

The Effectiveness of the St. Mungo Services

Follow-up of Men Leaving

Previously it was suggested that two criteria were available for evaluating the effectiveness of the St. Mungo houses. The first was relevant to the original aim of St. Mungo's, the resettlement of destitute men in independent accommodation. The effectiveness of St. Mungo's in achieving this aim could be assessed by a series of short-term follow-up enquiries and by an on-going follow-up of a cohort. The second criterion was relevant to the modified aim suggested by the research team and adopted by St. Mungo's after the pilot survey. This aim was the resettlement of men in St. Mungo houses. The extent to which this was achieved could be assessed by reference to the length of stay of men in houses.

A regular check on the whereabouts of men who had been resident in St. Mungo houses was made every two months by the research team. Information was gathered from St. Mungo workers and from the staff of other voluntary organisations and London reception centres. The follow-up check on the whereabouts of men resident in the Community on 1st January 1972 (N=35), and also on those men admitted during February 1972 (N=29), has been described previously. Only 5% of the men followed-up seemed to have changed from a completely disorganised or rootless way of life to something more settled, as a result of spending several months in St. Mungo houses.

Similar follow-up enquiries were made many times by the research team during the course of the project and the results were always very similar. For example, a regular check on the whereabouts of men who were resident

---

* The proportion of men staying in St. Mungo houses at least three months who said they had been in psychiatric hospitals doubled between April 1973 and April 1976 (from 20–39%).

in St. Mungo houses on 1st October 1972 was made every two months. There was very little change in the men's mode of life during the subsequent four years. By April 1976, 24 out of the 56 men in this group could not be traced (18 of these men had disappeared almost at once after a very brief stay). Of the rest, 25 were in accommodation provided by St. Mungo's, one man was in contact with the soup-run, one was in hospital, two were in Part III accommodation, and one had died. Only two men were living in their own accommodation.

Another group of 114 men admitted to St. Mungo houses between 1st October 1972 and 28th February 1973 was followed up, in the same manner, at two-monthly intervals until April 1976. A large proportion of these men could not be traced at all ($N=62$), leaving 52 men whose whereabouts were known. Of these, 23 men (including nine in the Marmite night shelter, and one in Lennox Buildings) were living in St. Mungo accommodation or had recently been in one of the houses. Seven men were in reception centres, three in hospital, and three in prison. Eleven men were squatting or sleeping rough and one had died. Two men were in their own accommodation, and two were in lodging houses.

Other follow-up enquiries did not allow a more optimistic assessment of outcome. It has been suggested that the shortest-term follow-up enquiry is the most complete and probably provides the best test of the efficiency of methods of rehabilitation (Wing, 1966).

Table 1. The number of men resident in the St. Mungo night shelters and houses on eight six-monthly census days from October 1972 to April 1976.

| | Shelters | | Houses | | |
	Marmite	St. Anne's	Available beds	Occupied beds	Occupancy %
7 Oct. 1972[a]	—	—	66	42	64
7 Apr. 1973	—	20	98	72	73
6 Oct. 1973	—	54	116	84	72
6 Apr. 1974	207	56	120	99	83
5 Oct. 1974	Closed	30	126	95	75
5 Apr. 1975	76	19	115	91	79
4 Oct. 1975	132	Closed	101	83	82
3 Apr. 1976	103	Closed	104	84	81

[a] The night shelter at St. Anne's had not yet opened.

Length of Stay

The expansion of the St. Mungo Community (see Table 1) is evident. The number of men in St. Mungo houses doubled by October 1973 and thereafter remained fairly constant. The number of house places varied as the houses were opened and closed (they were all short-lease properties); the bed occupancy in the houses was usually 75–80%.

Table 2. The number of men admitted to St. Mungo's houses during three consecutive one-year periods, and a final six-month period.

	First ever admission	Not first admission	Number of admissions	Staying at least 3 mth N	%
Oct. 1972—Sept. 1973	154	103	413	64	15·5
Oct. 1973—Sept. 1974	172	150	483	80	16·5
Oct. 1974—Sept. 1975	83	135	362	65	18·0
Oct. 1975—March 1976	39	28	75	38	50·7

Table 2 shows admissions of men to houses divided into men who had never been in a St. Mungo house before and readmissions during the period. Since each man might be admitted to houses several times, the total number of admissions during the period is also given. Finally, the table gives the number and proportion of admitted men who stayed in St. Mungo houses for at least three months.

During the period October 1972–September 1973, 413 men were admitted to St. Mungo houses, 64 of whom stayed for at least three months (15·5%). Of the 257 men admitted, 154 (59·9%) had not been in a St. Mungo house before. Thus there was a considerable turn-over of men without very much success in the way of resettlement following. The number of places available in houses was increasing during this period, and the St. Anne's night shelter catered for many of the men who wished to stay with St. Mungo's for only a short time (see Table 1). During the following year, out of 483 men admitted to houses, 80 (16·5%) stayed there for at least three months. During this period the Marmite night shelter was opened for a few months, the St. Anne's night shelter continued to operate and a few more house places became available. Since the numbers of men staying in houses three months or more were not increasing very much, the research team suggested a policy of early readmission of men discharged from the houses (see p. 59). During the third year, October 1974–September 1975, the policy began to have an effect, in that the numbers of first admitted men (most of whom were now admitted to the Marmite night shelter) began to decrease. Only 83 out of the 218 men admitted during this period (38%) had not used St. Mungo houses before. The total number of men admitted also went down, although the number of places available in the houses remained much the same. There was, however, little evidence that more men were settling in the St. Mungo houses. The proportion of men staying in houses three months or more increased slightly to 18% but the actual number of men went down compared with the previous year (from 80 to 65). During the six-month period, October 1975–March 1976, the referral procedure described previously was put into operation and this resulted in a sharp reduction in the number of men admitted to houses. (The figures shown for this period in Table 2 should be doubled in order to make them comparable with a full year.) On the other hand a much larger proportion of men (50·7%) stayed in houses for more than three months.

Table 3. The length of stay of the men in St. Mungo houses on successive census days, beginning with 1st October 1973 when the number of places available in the houses had approximately reached a plateau.

	0–3 mth	4–6 mth	7–9 mth	10–12 mth	>1 yr	TOTAL
Oct. 1973	45	6	13	5	15	84
Oct. 1974	38	9	12	6	28	93
Oct. 1975	35	5	1	6	31	78
Apr. 1976	20	18	11	5	30	84
Aug. 1976	4	11	11	4	44	74

The figures in Table 3 show that the number and proportion of men who had been resident in the houses for more than three months increased markedly after October 1975 (1st October 1973, 46·4%; 1st October 1974, 59·1%, 1st October 1975, 55·1%, 1st April 1976 76·2%; 13 August 1976, 94·6%). During the final months of the research project few men were admitted to the houses, since the places there were already occupied. It was apparent that unless many of the "long-stay" men (at the 13th August 1976 census, 44 of the 74 men in the houses had been resident there for a year or more) could be regarded as living in permanent accommodation, and other houses opened to accommodate men living in the Marmite night shelter, the movement of men from the night shelter to houses would rapidly come to a halt altogether.

Discussion

The St. Mungo action research project was designed in stages, each following on the one before. The initial stage of research comprised an evaluation of the effectiveness of the St. Mungo services that were operating at the time the research project began. When this pilot study was completed further stages of research had to be designed, since it had become apparent, through the research team's follow-up enquiries, that St. Mungo's was not succeeding in its aim of resettling, in independent accommodation, a large proportion of the destitute men admitted to its houses. The research team therefore suggested that a more restricted aim, that of inducing men to stay for long or indefinite periods in St. Mungo houses, should be substituted for that of the resettlement of men in independent accommodation. The St. Mungo management accepted this recommendation.

During the second stage of the project the research team advised St. Mungo's on methods of improving its services in order to better realise the new aim of resettlement. We made recommendations concerning the soup-run, staffing requirements and the improvement of the Community's day-to-day contact with destitute men, through day-time activities and a night-shelter. The establishment of a statistical register enabled any subsequent increase in the effectiveness of the St. Mungo services to be measured. In fact no increase in effectiveness occurred and the research team therefore decided to undertake a third stage of action research.

The third research stage differed from the first two in that specific changes in St. Mungo policies were recommended by the research team. The first recommended policy change was the early readmission of men leaving the St. Mungo houses. This change was implemented by the St. Mungo management but had no effect. An enquiry into the reasons why men left St. Mungo houses was therefore undertaken by the research team in order to obtain data that could be used as a basis for further suggestions. Two recommendations followed: the first was a modification of the no-drink rule; the second, a systematic assessment of the characteristics and the prospects of resettlement of men in the houses. The experience gained in this exercise, and the clarification of Community aims which it entailed, provided the foundation of a regular assessment procedure undertaken for all men seeking admission to St. Mungo houses from the Marmite night shelter. After this procedure began to operate the proportion of men settling in St. Mungo houses greatly increased.

During the final stage of the action research the research team was concerned with producing overall recommendations about the useful future development of the St. Mungo services on the basis of data collected during the project. It seemed clear to us that St. Mungo's was succeeding in attracting destitute men to settle in its houses and that this process, in the context of national provision of services for such men, ought to be encouraged.

The outcome of the St. Mungo project raised two related questions. The first concerned the reasons why destitute men eventually began to settle in St. Mungo houses. The second concerned the implications, for a policy of resettlement, of the situation facing the St. Mungo Community at the end of the research project. These questions are complementary and examine different aspects of resettlement. They will be considered in turn.

Two factors seemed to be responsible for the increased success of the St. Mungo services. The first was the new assessment procedure, the second the fact that the selection of men for houses was made from a night-shelter, rather than from the soup-run.

The assessment of men prior to house admission had become much more thorough than in previous years. The men's problems and the ability of St. Mungo's to help them were considered and particular care was taken to ensure that men were placed into an environment that seemed likely to be congenial to them. To this end the likely reaction of men to the residents and staff in particular houses was discussed.

The information necessary to make this procedure work was available because men were able to stay at the Marmite night shelter. The night shelter attracted large numbers of men. Admission on the first night was free (after the first night men were expected to register for benefit at a Social Security Office), entrants were not required to undergo a selection procedure, and the premises were so extensive (accommodating as many as 200 men) that men probably felt confident of getting a place and so were motivated to visit the night-shelter regularly. Because many men stayed at the Marmite night-shelter regularly (some every night) it was possible for night-shelter staff to maintain contact with them over a long period. In this way the more withdrawn men were eventually contacted. The Marmite night-shelter allowed more continuity of contact than the soup-run since men were available for contact over a longer period and there were full-time night-shelter staff who could regularly continue any contacts made. Men were now considered more systematically, whether they chose to ask for house admission or not. In these ways, the St. Mungo selection process probably came to resemble that followed at a reception centre, when men were selected for the residents' section.

The process of selection resulted in an accumulation of men in the St. Mungo houses who had experienced severe destitution; as many as half these men were also severely handicapped, the majority because of psychiatric illness or disability. The St. Mungo services did, therefore, achieve a degree of success. Men with a long experience of destitution were induced to change their way of life. On the whole this did not occur because of a process of "rehabilitation", but was due to a process of selection and the provision of options.

The research team had always envisaged that the criterion of success adopted as a result of the pilot survey (the resettlement of destitute men in St. Mungo houses) would eventually lead to the accumulation of a group of men who would fill all the house places available. If this occurred the provision of St. Mungo bed-sitters, with minimal supervision, would, to an extent, restore a flow of men through the houses, from the streets to a form of settled living. The problem of the severely handicapped residents in St. Mungo houses would, however, remain. It seemed that if these men were not to block all movement into St. Mungo houses from the Marmite night-shelter, one of two conditions would have to be met. Either St. Mungo's would have to acquire more houses or the handicapped residents in the Community's existing houses would have to be referred to other accommodation.

A policy that aims at the resettlement of destitute men assumes that appropriate accommodation is available in which these men can be resettled. Thus, the role of reception centres is stated to be that of providing temporary accommodation whilst arranging a variety of suitable longer-term placements for the men contacting them. This role is based on the belief that the destitute population is comprised of subgroups distinguished by the possession of particular needs and requiring the provision of specialised residential services (Ministry of Health, 1946).

The role of St. Mungo's, as formulated by its management at the time the research project began, was essentially the same as that of reception centres. However, both reception centres (statutory services) and the St. Mungo Community (a voluntary service perceived by its staff as a radical alternative to statutory provision) have faced a similar problem. Both kinds of agency have experienced an accumulation of residents in the absence of appropriate provision in the community for these men.

There is a lack of accommodation specifically intended for single people with low incomes and the numbers of rented rooms and lodging-houses (the traditional accommodation of the single low-paid worker) are declining (Wood, 1976). There is, in particular, a shortage of appropriate community provision for the handicapped. Thus, surveys of destitute men have suggested that gaps in mental hospital after-care facilities result in these men frequently relapsing after treatment, since, upon discharge from hospital, they are obliged to live in the unsettling environments of reception centres or common-lodging houses, or to sleep rough (Rollin, 1970).

It is against a background of gaps in community provision that the feasibility of a policy of resettlement should be assessed. The activities of agencies like the St. Mungo Community cannot be viewed in isolation from this wider social context. In part, the extent of their success in resettling destitute men reflects the priorities of their society. Page (1965), who worked at the Camberwell Reception Centre, wrote of the problems experienced by Centre staff in attempting to refer men living at the Centre to outside agencies:

> The local mental hospital is overloaded to resistance point; the local DRO* already hard pressed, has no hope of coping with the immense hidden employment problem; there are waiting lists ranging up to a year for most mental after-care hostels, alcoholic units, epileptic colonies and government training centres. Where are these men to wait, even supposing they are deemed "suitable"?

The workers of the St. Mungo Community faced the same predicament. Although it was the responsibility of the medical and social services to cater for the needs of the men living in the St. Mungo houses, appropriate provision

---

* Disablement Resettlement Officer. His role is to assist the disabled to find open employment if at all possible.

was not usually available in the community. There is often a reluctance, on the part of social service departments, to provide supervised accommodation for severely handicapped people. Most of the hostels provided for those who have been mentally ill, for example, are occupied by people who are not severely handicapped (Hewett *et al.*, 1975).

Two-thirds of the men in the St. Mungo houses were judged by the research team to need the kind of intensive help provided by the St. Mungo Community (approximately two workers per house of ten men), usually because of the severity of their impairments. Many of the men in the houses were not much good at routine day-to-day tasks such as cooking or cleaning, and some men needed considerable supervision even to prevent self-neglect. The workers were often involved in providing specific kinds of help to the men. Two residents with severe memory impairments, for example, had to have instructions written down for them before they went out if they were to find their way back to their houses.

Since alternative accommodation was not available for these men the only way the St. Mungo Community could help other destitute men with similar disabilities would be to open more houses. The money for expansion of this kind, however, was not available. A few St. Mungo bed-sitters (single rooms in houses where the workers lived out) were set up but St. Mungo's lacked the resources to substantially expand this service. Since about a third of the men in the houses could probably have moved into less supervised accommodation more men could have been admitted to houses from the Marmite night-shelter. This judgment could not be evaluated by the research team because an increase in provision had not occurred; however if it is corrrect it indicates how a stream of men could make progress from the streets.

The impasse which the St. Mungo Community faces illustrates a general dilemma. Those attempting to resettle destitute men have concluded that successful resettlement depends on the fulfilment of two different conditions. First, resettlement agencies that destitute men find acceptable and are willing to contact, must be established. Second, these agencies must have appropriate referral outlets for the men contacting them. Success in fulfilling the first condition, as the St. Mungo Community found, creates its own problems in the absence of the fulfilment of the second.

Acknowledgments

The research team are indebted to the Trustees, Director, and staff of the St. Mungo Community Trust for their collaboration in this research, and to the Department of Health and Social Security for its support.

During the pilot survey, Dr Justin Schlicht carried out psychiatric examinations and Dr Harry Dawson was responsible for the follow-up information and for compiling histories of the men. Mrs Seta Waller was responsible for the processing of data and the beginnings of the statistical register. Mrs Susan Pettigrew replaced Mrs Waller in November 1972, at first full-time and later part-time. She undertook the follow-up surveys. Miss Hazel Houghton helped with interviewing the men during the first main stage of the research, by courtesy of the Department of Health and Social Security. Miss Ruth Sousa and Miss Janice Nixon helped with the statistical analysis. Miss Joan Jenkins and Mrs Jackie Marshall acted as part-time clerical assistants. The research project was supervised by Professor J. K. Wing.

References

Hewett, S., Ryan, P. and Wing, J. K. (1975). Living without mental hospitals. *J. Soc. Pol.* **4** (4), 391–404.

Hyman, H. H., Wright, C. R. and Hopkins, T. K. (1962). "Application of Methods of Evaluation; Four Studies of the Encampment For Citizenship." University of California Press, Berkeley and Los Angeles.

Leach, J. and Wing, J. K. (in press). "Helping Destitute Men; Action Research with the St. Mungo Community Trust."

Leach, J. and Wing, J. K. (1978). The effectiveness of a voluntary service for helping destitute men. *Br. J. Psychiat.* **133**, 481–492.

Lodge-Patch, I. C. (1970). Homeless men—a London survey. *Proc. R. Soc. Med.* **63**, 437–441.

Marris, P. and Rein, M. (1967). "Dilemma of Social Reform, Poverty and Community Action in the U.S." Routledge and Kegan Paul, London.

Ministry of Health (1946). Public Assistance Circular 136/36, HMSO, London.

Page, P. (1965). Camberwell Reception Centre. *New Soc.* **5**, 18–21.

Priest, R. G. (1970). Homeless men; a USA–UK comparison. *Proc. R. Soc. Med.* **63**, 441–445.

Rollin, H. (1970). From patients into vagrants. *New Soc.* **15**, 90–93.

Tidmarsh, D. and Wood, S. M. (1972). "Camberwell Reception Centre; Summary of Research Findings and Recommendations." Department of Health and Social Security, London.

Wing, J. K. (1966). Social and psychological changes in a rehabilitation unit. *Soc. Psychiat.* **1**, 21–28.

Wing, J. K. (1973). Principles of evaluation. *In* "Evaluating a Community Psychiatric Service" (Wing, J. K. and Hailey, A. M., eds). Oxford University Press, Oxford.

Wood, S. M. (1976). Camberwell Reception Centre; a consideration of the need for health and social services of homeless single men. *J. Soc. Pol.* **5** (4), 389–399.

The Issue of Rehabilitation

DANNY LEVINE

Introduction

Talk of rehabilitation to most workers in the field of vagrancy and two reactions are likely. Either they resolutely fail to give you anything other than impressions of the success of their particular scheme or they firmly state that they are not wishing to impose their values on vagrants and have no wish to turn human beings into factory fodder. Some may hold a balanced position in the middle but they are heard less often and seem curiously discredited. This chapter is an attempt to set out some of the real rather than the phoney–rhetorical issues that too often lie hidden in all the talk about rehabilitation of vagrants and I strongly suspect many other groups too.

Before looking at the questions in detail I should make my own position clear. I do not think we can shelter behind vague figures if we are honestly trying to establish programmes of care, cure, rehabilitation, etc. Let us heed de Tocqueville (1959, pp. 22–23) in his writings over a century ago:

> When I was district attorney, the number of young offenders had become decidedly alarming. It was daily increasing at a frightening rate. A few people had the idea of establishing a house of correction to remedy this evil. This conception had incredible difficulty in taking root in the public mind. Now success has made it popular. There is now a fifth or sixth as many young offenders compared to five years ago.
> I.   Have you documentary proof to establish that last fact?
> He. No. But it is within my personal knowledge, and I can assure you of it!

On the issue of values, of which I shall say more later, Clifford (1968, p. 24) has castigated the "attitudes of most social work projects" in the field of

75

rancy which have their "preconditioned standards accepted as the right ones" and which seek to help "another set of people whose standards are seen as not right to change and come up to the acceptable conditions". This view (and there are many like it) seems little short of moral posturing which denies in my experience the reality of the interaction between the vagrant and the rehabilitation agency. We cannot pretend that we do not have or seem to have different values, though ironically many vagrants condemn the style of life of young social workers in far more moral terms than the other way around. For many men the agony of the homeless life is real and the tramp in the hedgerow is a far cry from the down and out on city streets. Such autobiographies or biographies that exist show this agony and the wish to be something better whatever the vagrants' public voice is saying (Straus, 1974). Agencies of rehabilitation simply by existing are making some statement about the homeless men. What they need to be debating is not whether they are simply upholders of middle class values but rather whether the men wish to use them and if so how honestly and intelligently that incredible act of trust by the individual vagrant can be made good rather than soured.

The Return to Society

With (such) aid, the skid-row man leaves almost any station on the loop cleaned up, sobered up, dried out, physically built up, psychologically investigated and "purged", perhaps spiritually renewed, and sometimes even occupationally placed.
However despite the hopeful pronouncements of the stations (agencies) and the rather elaborate programs to implement them, most skid row alcoholics eventually return to skid row, to heavy drinking and then back onto the loop, regardless of which was the last station visited.

Wiseman (1971, pp. 218–219) describes in graphic terms the reality facing the majority of vagrant alcoholics entering agencies of "rehabilitation" or "recovery". This reality must inevitably also be shared by social workers in such agencies: shared, or pushed to the back of the mind, half forgotten in the demands of the work and brought out and dusted, often ambivalently, either in moments of honest self-critical appraisal or in an attempt to justify the work against a background of poor results.

When reference is made in this chapter to rehabilitation or some allied process it should not be assumed that I do not accept that there are various stages or levels of rehabilitation. Clearly vagrants who are seriously physically handicapped or who are brain damaged or quite elderly will be aspiring to their own levels of rehabilitation ideally within the framework of statutory services available in theory to all. This may include residence in sheltered housing or employment in a sheltered workshop. It could be argued that for some men and women the limits in their rehabilitation process may be set because of an inherent limitation such as age or physical disability. Such limits are however always being questioned. The Peter Bedford Project (1976) recounts in its reports how homeless men officially described as "unemployable" can take the opportunity to live in more normal communities rather than large government reception centres and to work in ordinary employment rather than remain workless because of some official label. Similarly vagrants with the problem of epilepsy have now demonstrated the capacity to function more effectively than was once thought possible.

However, despite the cautionary and realistic note so far used, I believe it is also true to say that in several important areas of social disadvantage or disability the problems of rehabilitation are closely linked with entry or re-entry into "straight" society. Residential drug rehabilitation programmes have a "re-entry" stage, day centres for the single homeless focus on a "return to a more stable way of life", alcoholic rehabilitation agencies place an emphasis on holding down a job from a base of independent accommodation and ex-offender projects look for a non-deviant life-style with the most desirable goal being a return to "straight" society after a "bent" life.

It is my experience that many vagrants, alcoholic or not, do clearly share some of these larger goals, at least in part. Bahr (1971) claims: "if the characterisation of homelessness as a pathological condition and skid row as an unfortunate place to be were an expression of middle class morality, then the values of men on skid row would have to be classified as middle class". We must ask ourselves, therefore, why so few accepting society's norms and values are assimilated into society and why society in turn appears so unprepared to accept back the vagrant man or woman. That there is a deep mutual distrust seems unarguable, as is the fact that the structure of our society, apparently caring, and giving much weight to community care in principle is in fact so constructed that the caring becomes ranged in strict priority: thus crippled children, old and handicapped people or ex-servicemen are seen as more meriting society's concern than vagrants. It would however be simplistic to explain away failure of the majority of vagrants to lead a "normal" life (as it is commonly understood) purely in terms of two intractably opposed groups facing each other across a void of mutual incomprehension and hostility. Those factors are present in the situation, but I believe we should retrace our steps and ask two fundamental questions:

(i) What factors exist within the very rehabilitation process which may make the return to society a difficult goal for the individual client?

(ii) Can the goal of a return to society ever be achieved, other than to a limited extent, within the existing structure of rehabilitation agencies and the prevailing ethos of both the social work field and of the wider society? If it can, is it a desirable goal?

Later I will examine some of the issues which I believe are present in the rehabilitation process and which I believe compound the difficulties for both the agencies and the individuals. These issues are related to the first question. The second question is quite simply and depressingly related to a fundamental query about the capacity of agencies to absorb or initiate change where existing methods fail and alternative practices are clearly needed. It is depressing because there seems to be too little evidence of real desire for change as far as agency goals and expectations are concerned. Indeed "change" is a key word here for it is a goal for clients that is achieved by barely a handful—and also something that agencies find difficult or even impossible to do when looking at their own structures or practices. If agencies find it difficult to change or improve—even in simple organisational matters such as day to day planning—then the task of the individual to initiate change in himself might need to be attempted without too much expectation of assistance from such agencies.

The term "change" may necessarily have to be somewhat imprecise. It is however my experience that in written or verbal reports on men many social workers and doctors do use phrases like "Mr X will have to change considerably if he is to overcome his drinking problem". Everyone is too reluctant to spell out just what is entailed in the process of change. Whatever else I mean by the term I am not at any stage talking in terms of a cure of a specific problem. Rather I would see the approach to change as an "attempt to develop and integrate patterns of living where these have suffered major disruption" (Raush and Raush, 1968, p. 210).

The crux of the problem of change is the perennial way in which agencies and individuals adopt actions and strategies that fit short-term expediency rather than make long-term plans or formulate clear objectives and realistic goals. For example, the image of a residential project for vagrant alcoholics that concentrates on abstinence and "participation" on the part of the residents, coupled with a return to work and a progression through various stages of supported accommodation is a familiar one. A similar pattern for vagrants who do not have drink problems can also be observed and has the appearance of a long-term strategy with reasonably clear goals. I would argue, however, that the stages are expedients and serve mainly to alleviate some problems in the short term. There are few long-term strategies to assist in overcoming poor employment prospects, poor literacy standards, social or emotional isolation, housing needs, to increase self-sufficiency and confidence, foster interdependence without outright dependency and a host of often quite fundamental needs which would equip an individual to cope in a complex industrial society.

Two surveys of hostels bear out the main thrust of my argument. A study of 24 hostels for homeless ex-prisoners reported that while there was agreement on what was not being provided, there was less agreement on what was (Home Office, 1971, p. 58). It goes on to ask whether the hostel wardens are "trying to produce long-term change" or "provide a breathing space". Fundamentally it concludes that the aims of hostels are "ambiguous". More recently Otto and Orford (1978) have summarised the situation as follows: "lack of clarity, contradictions and misunderstandings over goals and methods seem to be the rule rather than the exception at small hostels". While small hostels have been put under the microscope rather more than some other rehabilitation agencies I do not believe that they are any more uncertain or confused, and the comments made here would apply across the board. It too often follows that because of the uncertainty of the agency's goals the relationship between professional and client is also frequently hazy, uncertain and ill-defined, or even worse the social worker may act in conflict with the agency's goals and so confuse the client still further. An agency that only aims to alleviate short-term problems may be unsatisfying to a worker who seeks to bring about long-term change in an individual who can then reasonably retort "I didn't come here to change my life but just to get off the streets". The reverse can also occur. An agency may have long-term goals but workers may find it easier to work on short-term measures that are less stressful for all concerned. As Otto and Orford (1978) comment: "relationships between the helpers and their clients are made, broken, and sometimes remade in an apparently haphazard fashion".

In the remainder of this chapter I would like to examine some issues within the context of the two questions posed above. In doing so, it is not my intention to be critical of individual agencies but to stress the point that these issues do exist to a greater or lesser extent in agency practice, in individuals' relationships with those agencies, and within the rehabilitation process.

The Rehabilitation Process

Rehabilitation is difficult to understand and hard to achieve. There are a number of factors which contribute to the problems of the process and I will attempt to deal with what in my experience are the main ones.

Confusion about what Constitutes Rehabilitation

I know of few workers within the vagrancy field who, when contemplating their work, do not ask the questions "rehabilitate to what?" or "what is rehabilitation?". Chambers' dictionary provides meanings of the verb and the meanings provide clues as to why there is such confusion: "rehabilitate v.t. to reinstate, restore to former rights, privileges, rights, rank etc.; to clear the character of; to bring back into good condition, working order, prosperity;

to make fit, after disablement, for making a living or playing a part in the world".

If the vagrant has not formerly had status, rights and privileges, one cannot reinstate or restore them. Restoring these rights (if that is possible) does not necessarily "clear the character". Often the vagrant will be brought back into good condition only to find that he cannot gain acceptance or his rights. The last part of the definition would seem at first sight to offer most hope, linked as it is to the work ethic and/or playing a part in the world (as a part of society). Workers and clients alike face contradictions in this area in that jobs are difficult to obtain, are often monotonous and of little interest to many men, work is often in potentially exploitative occupations, e.g. casual building and catering work, and does not feel anything like "playing a part in the world" to vagrant or social worker (except perhaps as a charade) and, in society's eyes has very low status.

Straus (1974, p. 206) in his biography of a homeless man quotes the subject's view of these low-grade occupations:

> Almost any bright and enterprising social worker . . . would suggest that I get a job as plongeur (French for dish washer). They have somehow confused the idea of a professional with that of washing dishes in their own houses. At different times I had two of these "dream jobs". . . . In the enumeration of the concomitants of the excessive use of alcohol, it was an oversight that caused me to overlook the fact that dishwashing is a tumorous excrescence on the derrière of alcoholism.

A more general study (Erlam, 1976, p. 11) recently concluded that "casual workers in the catering industry are paid poverty wages for jobs which are often obtained in circumstances and conditions appropriate to a cattle market". I would therefore suggest that because rehabilitation has so many meanings, often contradictory, to vagrants and social workers, to magistrates, to the Church and to the general public, it has become meaningless as a term in all except those cases where it is closely defined. Indeed the term frequently becomes interchangeable with reclaim, reform or even resurrect, which are even more value laden and all embracing.

Aspirations and Expectations—Who Decides?

Since it is fortunately illegal for agencies to kidnap vagrants and "rehabilitate" them, agencies have to rely on the men themselves coming forward, whether by self referral in response to publicity by the agency, through referral sources or through another institution. Both the agency and the man have aspirations and expectations and one might be forgiven for thinking that, if the two are matched, a reasonable basis for a working relationship would be established, the vagrant could then use the agency positively and the agency could give the man the most appropriate help. But as Otto (1978) has shown the problems of the whole referral process are many: "the selection process is intuitive and subjective, involves the making of evaluative judgements, and is reported by staff in terms suggesting much suspicion and mistrust. There is a definite clash of interests between the different parties in the negotiations over selection".

My view is also that the situation rarely arises where this matching takes place or the clash of interest, is fully recognised. Circumstances place the vagrant in the position of supplicant; he is likely to see his situation in simple terms i.e. needing accommodation, understanding and—possibly—help with his problems. The agency might well be—and often is—looking for a man with motivation to change his circumstances and can be suspicious of a person merely looking for what might be seen as "a good rest". The pressures are such that it is difficult for either party to accurately assess each other's needs. Are both parties' views and perception equally important? There is a strong case for saying that the vagrant's claim is greater because the process is there for his benefit, he makes the effort, he wins or loses, lives or dies. Yet the agency decides who to accept, and on what basis, makes the rules, has most of the power. As Apte (1968, p. 53) puts it "the warden (of a hostel) can give or withhold privileges which are intensely important to the resident including of course the vital 'privilege' of whether a man enters the agency in the first place". Under the circumstances it is surprising that no noticeable vagrant self-help group has emerged, the counterpart of concept based movements in the offender and drug field such as the Delancy Street Foundation in San Francisco (Hampden-Turner, 1976). The problems of creating reforming organisations with the involvement of the vagrants themselves have been commented on by Mathiesen (1974, p. 106) though in the Scandinavian context: not least of the initial difficulties was the tendency of the vagrants to "disrupt the meetings"! But there are also more deep seated problems in trying to engender any form of self-help organisation among vagrants. They have after all been expelled from society partly because of their lack of contribution and efforts are made to invite them to contribute as a group, mainly one suspects because the well-paid professionals can come up with no "answer" to the problem of rehabilitation. But the homeless person's vulnerability is such that it seems to me that they fear any "militant" action on their part may remove the tenuous foothold they presently have in society, albeit at the very margins.

Adjusting to a Non-vagrant Life

Archard (1975) has challenged the view of the vagrant alcoholic as an inadequate by illustrating how, in order to lead a vagrant life, a man displays resourcefulness, makes relationships within the skid-row culture and develops mechanisms which will enable him to survive. How does he then adjust to a non-vagrant life and what are the areas of difficulty he might experience? Whatever type of institution or agency he chooses as his escape route from a vagrant state he will, to varying degrees, be expected to—and he might himself expect this—be stable, earn a living, take responsibility (at least for himself, if not for others), cope with a different time scale to that afforded by a vagrant life, acquire social skills, survive setbacks, increase self-confidence, be honest, abstain from his past deviance (not drink, not steal etc.), acquire leisure interests and develop to the point of obtaining non-supported accommodation. The implication here is that there are a large number of major areas in his life which he might be expected to work at in order to fundamentally change his circumstances—a formidable undertaking for anyone.

Thus the dilemma in the process of rehabilitation is how to tackle such vital areas of change and how to measure progress along the way. A simple statement that measurement should be in the client's terms can bring us up against the problem of agency needs. For example, a former vagrant alcoholic may not be drinking and may be taking some responsibility in a hostel but may not have any desire to work and may be socially isolated. How is his progress to be judged and by whom? Equally the changes needed, represent a considerable challenge to the fortitude of the client and require a high degree of skill and training for the social worker. If the task is approached on too broad a front there is a danger that little will be achieved; if slowly built up there is a danger that other factors will intrude. For example, if the vagrant wants to gain a work skill and obtain a place on a Government training scheme with a six month waiting list he may be angry that he has to wait for six months, wanting to see a change in his situation sooner, or alternatively his confidence may ebb just before the course starts and he may retreat. On the next time around the rehabilitation circuit his efforts may well then be coloured by what he has come to see as his previous failure to obtain an employment skill.

Time is a key area of adjustment to which little attention has been given. The difficulties of adapting to "sober time" and filling in the hours that have been formerly spent drinking on skid row have been accurately described by Wiseman (1971). It is a familiar experience to social workers to observe the difficulties former vagrants experience in structuring their time, adjusting to long hours formerly occupied by queueing, walking the streets, "wheeling and dealing" to obtain drink and by drinking. Meeting obligations to arrive punctually at work after, possibly, years of unemployment, is or can be, a demanding change just in itself. The problem of coping with time is a familiar one to many who have never experienced a vagrant life whether one is being asked to adjust to enforced inactivity or to increase activity to meet unaccustomed work or time demands. But in addition vagrant alcoholics talk about having "wasted" their lives up to now and wanting to catch up with the things they have missed. Thus they become impatient at delays and, reasonably in their terms, expect to see fairly immediate improvements in their situation once abstinence has been achieved.

The vagrant alcoholic needs to learn to cope with another dimension of the rehabilitation process, namely a life without drink. Indeed in very simple terms his success or failure in residential rehabilitation facilities is measured by whether or not he maintains sobriety, for relapse generally results in his departure. This situation obtains in the vast majority of facilities in England and Wales. The abstinence principle is one which provides a source of strength to many men and I would not wish to argue a case here for its abandonment. What concerns me about its prominent place in the rehabilitation process is that it is an external control i.e. it is virtually a condition of residence which is imposed on the man (the fact that the man may want the condition is not material to the argument). If the rehabilitation process does not assist the man to increase his own self confidence and ability to survive on his own in the longer term without drink, the move to independent accommodation will carry an extra threat to stability in that the control will have to be internal i.e. from within the man and not from the rules of the house. With the rate of relapse being high, there would not seem to be much evidence that men are acquiring the kind of confidence needed to make the switch from external to internal control. Ogbourne and Smart (1974, p. 17) state that "only a minority of clients complete the course" in alcoholic hostels. This point, as with so many others I have made, depends on an appreciation of the *ad hoc* nature of successful rehabilitation. Cook (1975, pp. 138–139), in an assessment of the Alcoholics Recovery Project, put it thus:

> (for example) a number of men have "failed" while with us, but the knowledge gained of them and their continuing relationship with us has enabled us to place each man in another centre more appropriate to his needs and where he has flourished. Conversely, of course, some of the men whom we might list as "successes" are only such because of what they have learnt in other settings prior to coming to us.

Even with this caveat the "success" rates are still on everyone's admission small.

Confidence does not only relate to drinking controls. Men in the rehabilitation process have invariably had souring experiences with statutory and voluntary agencies and with various institutions and individuals. They therefore tend to be mistrustful and lack the confidence which would enable them to place their trust in others and cope reasonably if their trust proves misplaced. How far along the rehabilitation road is a man who has been abstinent for several years but still views, say, shopkeepers with deep suspicion and becomes very aggressive and tense if he suspects that they are cheating him (justifiably or not)? One could argue that he is still seriously at risk, abstinence notwithstanding.

"Going straight" is another factor in the rehabilitation process which can place a man under pressure. The process demands that a man be honest and he expects others to be the same. The shopkeeper thought to be cheating the customer, social security paying late or at the wrong rate, the extent of industrial theft, people generally not keeping their word, lack of consistency in word and action on the part of the social worker, all these induce feelings of resignation, cynicism or outrage among men in rehabilitation houses and projects. It is not easy to approach life honestly and directly after years of deviousness and imprisonment; it feels like a tremendous effort for some, and is. For others, honesty is the norm instilled in childhood by a Calvinist upbringing and sustained over a long period despite imprisonment, drink and a vagrant life-style. Truth is truth, lies are lies. Some men do tend to be intolerant of rehabilitative attempts to define truth and untruth in "realistic" relative terms because it sounds like an evasion. These men live by absolute standards and so, they say, should others. It is worth noting that Orford (1974) found such simplistic thinking a clear bar to progress in a rehabilitation hostel and saw success in some respects developing as a resident became more cognitively complex. One drug rehabilitation agency, operating by strict rules of individual responsibility and honesty, uses the "re-entry" (to society) period to help men cope with a society which is less honest than the community in which they have been living!

This last point raises the important questions of values and standards and, once more, who decides what constitutes realistic goals. Archard (1975) states that the normative standards are set by society—job, leisure activities, family relationship—and reflect the values of the society. The rehabilitation process recognises the fact by stating implicitly or explicitly that these objectives are desirable. Redl (1959) refers to the "value system that oozes out of our pores". Thus we apparently have objectives against which agencies or individuals can measure progress. Yet it is against these criteria that the majority of vagrants tend to fare badly. Does the reabilitation process, therefore, seek to achieve targets which are too difficult for a man to attain or—perhaps more to the point—which he might not want since he might measure his own progress by different criteria. The point is not only an important one in its own right but seriously impinges on another aspect of the rehabilitation process, namely perceptions of what consitutes failure and how to cope with it.

Social workers in my experience, do not often contemplate rehabilitation in this field in terms of failure. Successes are acknowledged but failures are not. Jansen (1970) noted in community mental health programmes the "discrepancies between write-ups and actual practices". In some ways this is bound to occur because who is to say that a man has failed simply because he left an agency either before the workers thought he should or because of relapse? If we regard the rehabilitation process as potentially having a cumulative beneficial effect, then each experience can be seen as having a positive element within it. This can of course lead to justifying every kind of "failure" as temporary and redefining it as a "learning experience" (more often for the worker rather than the client). Some men do see "failure" in such terms. Others see the experience in a negative light expressing a considerable sense of failure and guilt, rarely about failure to obtain work or achieve other similar objectives related as they see it to "normal living", but more usually about the relapse itself. Expressions such as "I've done it all wrong" or "I've let you down" are common and some men have implied that they could not face their former fellow residents if they relapsed, particularly if it occurs after a long period of abstinence.

If the worker does not see relapse as failure but the vagrant does, it is clearly the vagrant's own perception which is the more important for him. The relapse may well follow an earlier sense of failure experienced by not obtaining a job or failing in some other way to respond appropriately to the rehabilitation setting. Equally the rehabilitation agency may have failed the man or may seek to convince him that he has failed because, for example, the resident does not want to work. In the area of mutual expectations and what constitutes success and failure there appears to be considerable confusion, particularly with regard to whose are the dominant perceptions.

Rehabilitation—An Ordinary Process

The view has been expressed that the rehabilitation process should be regarded as extraordinary and that the process would be enhanced if it could be seen as more ordinary, thus reducing the stress and the pressure to "do well". How ordinary or extraordinary is the process?

I would submit that it is extraordinary in that it tends to reveal a whole range of "defects" in an individual's situation or personality: a shopping list of what must be put right before everything comes good. Thus people can be ruthlessly exposed, particularly in the intensely therapeutically orientated agency, and the freedom to be a "mess" in some areas of one's life is denied. Contrast this with, say, a shared house where no one is labelled as having a socio-medical problem or whatever and the tolerance level towards the individual's ability or inability to cope with life is high.

It is extraordinary in that some people are labelled "helper" and the others "helped". It is extraordinary in the sense that the vagrant men are potentially looking at areas of their lives which others take for granted. They are also involved in making conscious changes whereas the great majority of society

D

regress, stay the same, develop or—more rarely—try to change. Even if they do it may be largely unconscious and rarely in the semi-public gaze.

It is extraordinary that the very problem of forming relationships is not infrequently used as a reason for not admitting someone to a facility that in theory is to enable someone to form those relationships, an essential factor in any so called rehabilitation process. It is extraordinary that so often there is little or no integration between the agency and the "outside" world so that there is a considerable dislocation on leaving the agency, which often occurs in a crisis. As Otto and Orford (1978) comment it is at the point of departure that "people are cut off from the sources of socialising influence and from their newly found position of partial social integration".

It is extraordinary in that there is an attempt to increase the vagrant's ability to relate to others from a base of largely male orientated residential facilities and this often against a background of having experienced single-sex institutions for many years. So, I would argue that the process is extraordinary but that it ideally seeks to achieve the extraordinary in the most relaxed ordinary circumstances possible. The fact that there is a panoply of workers, institutions and welfare systems around cannot really help to foster a feeling of ease but that seems inevitable at present.

The Agency and Society—Help or Hindrance?

Plainly there are a proportion of people achieving a "return to society" at present via existing rehabilitation agencies. It should also be remembered that some agencies and institutions do not see themselves or, more importantly, are not perceived as having that goal, e.g. casual stay at government reception centres, common-lodging houses, some day and night shelters or prison, with the result that men using those facilities tend to be maintained at a minimum level. A further but unknown number of people achieve the goal without the help of any agency. What concerns me is the first group of agencies, whose stated intentions are usually to assist the man to return to, or be accepted by, society as an ordinarily valued member through the process referred to earlier.

In the opening paragraph of the chapter I referred, apparently dismissively, to the fact that agencies are not too interested in, or capable of, change. All agencies I know of are interested in improving their performance and increasing the effectiveness of their work. Where I do think agencies have great difficulty is in determining how to modify, or radically depart from, existing practice so as to be more effective. All agencies become locked to a lesser or greater extent in their own history and practices and thus find change difficult. They become prisoners of their own programmes. Paradoxically, change might be even more difficult in those agencies where the relationship is most comfortable between professional and clients since such agencies tend to be cherished by their clients for what the agencies are and have been and there is a certain expectation that things will continue in roughly the same way. But all the agencies have typically 80% or more clients returning to a vagrant or recidivist life-style. The agencies appear to the clients to be remarkably similar whatever the different agencies themselves feel or say about their philosophies, styles and regimes.

The relationships between professional and client, too, present difficulties in terms of their respective situations in life, the relative lack of experience of many of the professionals, ambivalence on the part of the vagrants towards the professionals, or the actual implementation of the rehabilitation programme.

Agencies often appear remarkably ill-equipped to carry out their tasks, being under resourced, politically weak and often unclear about their practical objectives. They operate in the margins of statutory activity, under great pressure and, necessarily, because of financial constraints must confine themselves to attempting to assist only a small proportion of people in need of help.

What is done well in some cases is to help the individual clients focus on their particular problem areas, but this approach tends to prioritise the task of rehabilitation as being to overcome the inadequacy and recidivism of the vagrant over and above that of influencing the professionals and institutions and the society the vagrant seeks to enter or re-enter. Some might say that that is a true reflection of the priorities but I would argue that the first without the second provides a serious obstacle to the vagrant's re-entry to society. Again, if agencies insist that all they can realistically consider is the first approach, I would argue that insufficient choice exists for the vagrant as to regime, existing regimes are not flexible enough, insufficient attention is paid to ensuring that agency and client have similar expectations of the rehabilitation process, and little if any forward planning takes place.

I wish to examine briefly some of the issues inherent in a consideration of this relationship between the rehabilitation agencies and society at large.

The Indeterminate Sentence

One complaint of recidivists is that, whilst a prison sentence is of fixed duration, even subject to remission for good behaviour, the period after release more closely resembles an indeterminate sentence in society, not accepted by employers or neighbours, not knowing what will please and when the "sin" of the prison will be expiated. So it is with vagrants seeking re-entry with stigmatisation and mistrust clinging, for an unknown period. I recall a public meeting in support of a planning application to open a hostel for vagrant alcoholics where a colleague of mine, himself formerly a vagrant alcoholic, sober for three years, explained his own previous circumstances and how projects such as the one we proposed could bear similar fruit. At the subsequent planning committee hearing, a councillor who had been present at the public meeting opposed our application stating scornfully that one of the staff "by his own admission" was a former vagrant alcoholic! It should be borne in mind here that our staff member had a considerable number of social advantages being an eloquent speaker in a socially accept-able job and was still the subject of prejudicial and inappropriate comment.

Social Priorities

I am not qualified to give a sociological perspective of the place to which society consigns its vagrants or to the societal causes of vagrancy. However, as a practitioner in the field one has views and a rule of thumb guide to atti-tudes towards the vagrants. Public utterances tend to be made by those vociferously opposed to the vagrant, viewing him as a parasite of the Welfare State. One does not know what the great mass of the population feels about him apart from knowing vagrants are an unpopular cause (Norris, 1978). One might reasonably guess it from such recent studies as "The Perception of Poverty in Europe" where the view of 43% of the British population is that poverty occurs because of laziness and lack of willpower (Commission of European Communities, 1977, p. 72). This contrasts markedly with Denmark for example where only 11% held this view.

When it comes to the allocation of central and local government resources to agencies in the field, the position is clearer. Archard (1975) reports a social worker stating that "if there existed a pop-chart of . . . concern for social problems, then vagrant (alcoholics) would probably always remain at the bottom". The reality of this view is borne out by the research report on male offenders which looked particularly at homeless offenders, both vagrants and more transient homeless. On probation officers' attitudes to the homeless offenders the report declared: "the other's attitudes towards homeless clients and the feelings of frustration they experienced in dealing with them were accurately summarised in the words of one of them who said '. . . whilst I am always willing to go on trying with homeless men, I am glad for the sake of my morale that I also have other more hopeful cases to deal with' " (Home Office, 1975, p. 39). But what is more alarming is when vagrants do not appear at all on anyone's list. For example, in all the recent announcements coming from the Department of the Environment about plans to halt urban decay in the Inner City and in all the subsequent local authority activity no mention at all has been made about the Inner City vagrant population and that they even exist let alone might figure in plans to mobilise more resources.

Where have all the Programmes Gone?

Given that the present range of agencies and institutions exist and have a job to do, it should follow that some sort of programmes, presumably with various permutations, would exist to assist the rehabilitation process. Equally, given the high rate of unemployment among vagrants in rehabilitation facilities, one would assume that ways would be explored to help men cope with long periods of leisure time.

The notion of a programme is crucially related to rehabilitation as a process not as a once and for all event. Agencies may boldly state that it is a process, but then seem to do everything to indicate a tendency to treat it as a once and for all event. The short-term gains are all too familiar and all too easily colluded with by the agencies. "Every day out of prison is a success" is dramatic in its appeal but may contain within it the wilful ignoring of some much needed long-term planning to aid the process.

Programmes as such do not enjoy much popularity in the field at the moment. Support, informal counselling and periodic group meetings of a non-psychotherapeutic nature are mainly the preferred means of assisting the rehabilitation process. One must ask whether that system allows for sufficient internal structure, a source of strength for people attempting to change. Again, while such structures might be fairly low key, is there not a place for some modest attempt at a more highly structured programme or even separating accommodation needs from the rehabilitation programme? In this latter case I am thinking of a situation where, for example, vagrants could have access to a good standard of accommodation in non-institutional houses e.g. an independent flat, whilst undergoing a daily rehabilitation programme elsewhere. The flat or room could then be available on a normal tenancy basis governed only by the normal rules of a tenancy, and not have the tenancy incorporated into the rehabilitation process with all the dangers that it entails if there is a breakdown.

With regard to leisure activities, some time ago I received a request from Sweden to say what proportion of resources and staff time were devoted to promoting good use of leisure time within agencies dealing with vagrants. Upon enquiring I found that, like myself, very few agencies had given much thought to the subject. Yet in our society generally the subject of how one uses one's leisure time is regarded as being very important. In my own case, I felt inhibited from intervening in this area since it was plain that my perception of appropriate use of leisure time and that of the men with whom I was working was vastly different. The question was side-stepped then, but cannot continue to be avoided since such a high proportion of men in rehabilitation facilities are unemployed and the need for structuring time is so clear (Wiseman, 1972).

Life Begins at 40

As the majority of vagrant men are middle aged, the well-known words of the song, and the acceptance of the dictum in modern mythology, carry a message of hope that all is not lost, that it is still possible to make something of one's life at that age. As the vagrant moves on towards the late 50s, however, agency views begin to change perceptibly, particularly if the man is in indifferent health (Wood, 1976). In the case of poor health the question of the amount of staff time potentially tied up nursing him becomes a factor in whether to admit a man to a rehabilitation facility. In the case of physical disability, legislation forbids certain hostels from accommodating such a person above the ground floor and as the bedrooms are usually on the first floor and higher, admission is again problematic.

So, life *can* begin at 40 and for many of the "lucky 20%" actually does. It would, however, be idle to pretend that age cannot pose problems. It certainly can in the field of employment, where competition is fierce even among people without the social disability and stigma of having been a vagrant. This is particularly true when entering an occupation different to that in which you have normally been employed, e.g. the alcoholic moving from catering work to factory or office work. It must be easier for those with status in their former occupation to move to a new field, particularly if they can be self employed in the new field of work.

The clear implication of the "life begins at 40" statement is that it is possible if a person is adventurous enough to want to try. Once more we have to return to the recurring theme of "what kind of a life," and "who decides?"

The Return to Society as a Desirable Goal

I should begin by stating that I consider that whether or not a return to society is a desirable goal it is a necessary one. I consider the "leading a more stable life" goal to be a substitute not an alternative. A return to society is necessary because it implies belonging, relating to those around one in a mutually supportive way and growth within the mainstream of society.

The fact that so few attain it, however, might well bring into question its desirability: for some the attraction of a desired objective *is* its very unattainability. We must also ask ourselves what price the vagrant is required to pay to attain such a necessary or desirable state: he most certainly will have to exercise more self discipline than the average citizen, he will be in situations perhaps for years where he is uncomfortable and unconfident, he will use an agency—probably several—who might well be uncertain about how to advise him, about their relationship to him, possibly even unsure about their own views on the merits of the society in which we live. He will relapse—possibly many times—and face rejection, think that he has "arrived" and find that he has not. So why bother, and are the results worth the effort? I feel that they are, in so far as the society we have is the *only* one we have, and it will change very slowly. It cannot at present, and for the foreseeable future, adapt well to people living outside its mainstream. Therefore it tends to reward those who are within, and be punitive towards those outside. The vagrant knows the latter position well because it conditions and influences his rootless life.

What we do not know is the best route(s) through the rehabilitation process in order to achieve the goal, how a wider choice of routes can be made available, and how the vagrant can be given more power on the way so as to exert a greater influence on the agencies and society of which he seeks to be a part. At present any movement by a vagrant tends to be "round in circles" rather than "onwards and upwards" (Otto and Orford, 1978) mainly because we have failed to face the issues involved in going onwards and upwards. We manage the circles much better.

One way in which some have advocated that those outside society might really find their place in it is to take up a "new career" as a helper rather than remain one of the helped. The new careers movement has been considerable in the USA but much less so in England. One area that neither country seems successfully to have tackled is a new careers scheme involving former vagrants as opposed to men who have had occasional bouts of homelessness. I was involved for a substantial period of time with one such scheme in England. A few difficulties that were encountered might serve to illustrate how long term and unbelievably complex the thing we call rehabilitation really is.

I was given the responsibility to recruit, train and then manage a team of four former vagrant alcoholics so that together we could establish a network of new experimental facilities for vagrants. In the process the team of four would gain skills and experience that could launch them on a new career.

A number of issues arose in the course of this project that deserve mention for the illustrations they provide of the problems previously raised. A key problem was the time scale in that the structuring of time on the scheme became an area of great tension: discussing a course of action was a waste of time as what was needed was action. Early rewards were needed. Too much time had been lost and too few rewards obtained in the vagrant way of life. This led on to another vital area, namely what counted as "real work". It was practical work that was needed, not planning how the facilities might best operate and what was appropriate. This problem was complicated by the definite but simplistic thinking that tended to dominate the discussions making progress for both individuals and the project difficult.

Finally my own time scale was at fault in seriously underestimating the difficulties and time required to change from the role of helped into that of

helper. To move at all from the role of helped is arduous, as I believe I saw
when one or two of the "new careerists" relapsed and almost overnight became clients again. Old well-tried roles are always the easiest for all of us and
the former vagrants were no exception. It was sad to see how near the surface
the "client" often was. I say this not in any condemnatory sense but out of
regard for the courage and determination that seems to be required for any
"outsider" to re-enter society. It is of no conceivable service to anyone to
underestimate the value of that re-entry or the long journey that it entails.

References

Apte, R. Z. (1968). "Halfway Houses", Occasional Papers on Social Administration,
    No. 27. Bell, London.
Archard, P. (1975). "The Bottle Won't Leave You." Alcoholics Recovery Project,
    London.
Bahr, H. (1973). "Skid Row: An Introduction to Disaffiliation." Oxford University
    Press, Oxford.
Clifford, W. (1968). "The Simon Scene." Housman, London.
Commission of the European Communities (1977). "The Perception of Poverty in
    Europe." Brussels.
Cook, T. (1975). "Vagrant Alcoholics." Routledge and Kegan Paul, London.
de Tocqueville, A. (1959). "Journey to America" (Mayer, J. P., ed.). Faber,
    London.
Erlam, A. and Brown, M. (1976). "Catering for Homeless Workers." CHAR and
    Low Pay Unit, London.
Hampden-Turner, C. (1976). "Sane Asylum." San Francisco Book Co., California.
Home Office (1971). "Habitual Drunken Offenders." HMSO, London.
Home Office (1975). "Some Male Offenders' Problems." HMSO, London.
Jansen, E. (1970). The role of the halfway house in community health programmes
    in the United Kingdom and America. Am. J. Psychiat. 126, 1498–1504.
Mathiesen, T. (1974). "The Politics of Abolition." Martin Robertson, London.
Norris, M. (1978). Those we like to help. New Soc. 45 (822), 18.
Ogbourne, A. C. and Smart, R. E. (1974). "Halfway Houses for Skid Row
    Alcoholics: A Search for Empirical Evaluation." Addiction Research Foundation,
    Toronto.
Orford, J. (1974). Simplistic thinking about other people as a predictor of early
    drop-out at an alcoholism halfway house. Br. J. Med. Psychol. 47, 53–62.
Otto, S. and Orford J. (1978). "Not Quite Like Home." J. Wiley, London.
Peter Bedford Project (1976). Annual Report, 76 Liverpool Road, London.
Raush, H. L. and Raush, C. L. (1968). "The Halfway House Movement—A Search
    for Sanity." Appleton-Century-Crofts, New York.
Redl, F. (1959). The concept of a therapeutic milieu. Am. J. Orthopsychiat. 29,
    721–35.
Straus, R. (1974). "Escape From Custody." Harper and Row, New York.
Wallich-Clifford, A. (1968). "The Simon Scene." Housman, London.
Wiseman, J. P. (1971). "Stations of the Lost: The Treatment of Skid Row
    Alcoholics." Prentice-Hall, New Jersey.

Wiseman, J. P. (1972). Sober time: the neglected variable in the recidivism of alcoholic persons. 2nd Annual Alcoholism Conference of National Institute on Alcohol Abuse and Alcoholism, Washington, USA.
Wood, S. M. (1976). Camberwell Reception Centre: a consideration of the need for health and social services of homeless, single men. *J. Soc. Pol.* **5** (4), 389–399.

Vagrancy and the Criminal Law

LEONARD LEIGH

Introduction

An account of the vagrancy laws must necessarily be prefaced by certain explanations. When a lawyer speaks of vagrancy and the vagrancy laws he does not invoke precisely defined concepts. Furthermore, he is apt not to mean the same thing as his colleagues in the other social sciences who, in any event, tend to use the phrase "homeless single person". That phrase, deriving from a report by the National Assistance Board (1966), signifies itinerant persons, either single or effectively single, using accommodation provided for transients. It has been likened to a flag of convenience denoting a disparate body of persons including the vagrant, the causal labourer, the itinerant navvy, the mentally ill, the physically disabled, and the old-age-pensioner with no family ties (Stewart, 1975). The term "vagrant" carries, and always has carried, pejorative connotations. It signifies persons from whom, it is thought, criminal conduct is to be anticipated. The Vagrancy Act 1824 and certain related statutes are directed towards criminality rather than poverty as such. Of course certain offences, in particular sleeping rough, apply in practice to indigent persons, but poverty and homelessness are not offences. Most of the offences under the statute are directed towards the prevention of crime or the elimination of certain nuisances.

The structure of the Vagrancy Act 1824 derives from the use of the criminal law to suppress the able-bodied vagrants and itinerant persons of supposedly criminal propensities stigmatised as rogues, vagabonds, and sturdy beggars.[1] This class has disappeared. The Vagrancy Act 1824 has

---

[1] *Ledwith* v. *Roberts* [1937] 1 K.B. 232.

not. It has been used generally for crime prevention. Its utility in crime prevention in no way depends upon any proposition that itinerants and alcoholics are inherently likely to commit crimes. Such persons are not specified as the objects of the statute nor are the principal provisions justified in relation to them.[2] The Vagrancy Act 1824 has, however, a substantial impact upon itinerant and indigent persons and so have the provisions of certain related statutes such as the Licensing Acts, the Mental Health Act 1959, and the Supplementary Benefits Act 1976.

Before attempting to discuss the history and the present state of the vagrancy laws it is perhaps desirable to outline some aspects of the problems associated with homeless single persons. The literature is at once voluminous and fragmented because it proceeds from persons studying different aspects of the problem. Habitués of Reception Centres differ in their characteristics from the inhabitants of crypts. Many persons prefer lodging houses to Reception Centres because of their distrust of bureaucracy. Certain classes of person, particularly alcoholics, are excluded from accommodation (National Assistance Board, 1966, para. 54; Holloway, 1970). In short, the typical profile of the user of one class of accommodation may not correspond very precisely with that of another. Nonetheless, certain generalisations do apply. In most groups of itinerants studied there is a high incidence of physical complaints, mental disorder (not necessarily falling within a category warranting admission to hospital under the Mental Health Act 1959) and alcoholism (Stewart, 1975, pp. 104–118). The Home Office Report (1971, para. 5. 21) concludes that schizophrenia is uncommon, but that depressive illness is not. What common and uncommon signifies in statistical terms is not stated. The research reports done for the Home Office state that there is no clear evidence from the studies as to how often severe mental illness which is not related to drink is to be found among drunkenness offenders. A substantial number of men are apprehensive of officialdom. As a result, many do not make use of the social security system (Archard, 1975, p. 53). A sizeable proportion have criminal records. There seems no reason to suppose that any pattern of commission of serious offences can be demonstrated. On the contrary, most offences are trivial such as petty theft or fraudulently attempting to obtain social security benefits of one kind or another (Stewart, 1975; McWilliams, 1975, pp. 10–11). Some persons are of course simply itinerant and in search of work, in some measure victims of a difficult housing situation (National Assistance Board, 1966, para. 270).

The disparate groups bracketed under the denomination of homeless single persons are on the whole representative neither of marauding bands of criminals, nor of young, work-shy wastrels whose chosen way represents a romanticised desire to opt out of the rigours of normal life. The young

---

[2]   *R.* v. *Jackson* [1974] 1 Q.B. 517 at p. 522 *per* Scarman L. J.

unemployed itinerant is, according to the literature, more likely to be immature, unskilled, and of low intelligence (Holloway, 1970). These are matters of importance in discussing the administration of the vagrancy laws. Before doing so, however, it is necessary to refer to the history of the vagrancy laws and to describe the structure which they retain to this day.

History

I do not propose to attempt an extensive account of the history of the vagrancy laws. Several admirable treatments already exist (Holdsworth, 1924; Chambliss, 1969; Langbein, 1976). It is perhaps enough to say that a mass of punitive legislation of considerable severity, not to say ferocity, was consolidated in the Vagrancy Act 1824. The provisions of the 1824 Act are diverse. It was directed at persons considered to be criminals; itinerants who would not work, wanderers thought to be of criminal tendencies, gypsies who practised fortune-telling, and prostitutes who solicited publicly. The poor laws existed for the relief of the deserving poor. The Vagrancy Acts were the answer to problems posed by unmeritable wanderers. Like so many simple solutions, this one failed to work and vagrancy did not disappear. In 1868 Sir John Lambert (1869. p. 34), a Commissioner of the Poor Laws, wrote:

> We have made fresh laws with each succeeding reign, and tried every species of cruelty, except, as Dr. Burn says, scalping. We have put these vagrants in the stocks for three days and three nights with only bread and water. We have stripped them naked and beaten them at the cart tail with whips, in market towns, until their bodies were bloody. For a second offence we have put them in the pillory and cut off one of their ears, and for the third offence we have cut off the other ear too. Next, by way of variety, we have excised the upper part of the gristle of the right ear, as we would deal with a terrier dog, and if they have sinned again, after this mild caution, we have condemned them as felons. With hot wax we have branded their bodies with several of the letters of the alphabet; and made them slaves, to be sold and disposed of as goods or cattle. At a later period we have caused them to be grievously whipped and burnt through the gristle of the right ear with a hot iron of the compass of an inch; and for a third offence we have hung them, as we would a murderer. Subsequently, we have resorted again to the practice of whipping, with the addition of transportation, or perpetual consignment to the galleys. Later on, we have abandoned the whipping and the other cruelties which I have just described, and now we are content to use the milder discipline of the treadmill or the tramp ward.

Despite the failure of the Vagrancy Acts they remain, restrictively amended, in our law to this day. Furthermore, they were exported to other countries such as the United States and Canada where they have been much eroded (Sherry, 1960) and to Australia where they seem to flourish in a state of pristine vigour (Sackville, 1976).

Structure

The vagrancy laws are, as I have suggested, directed against conduct which Parliament has declared to be criminal. Three broad categories are involved. The first might be called acquisitive crime and comprehends such offences as loitering with intent to commit an indictable offence, being found on enclosed premises for any unlawful purpose, begging, fortune-telling, and palmistry. A second category is directed towards public nuisances. The most prominent such offence is sleeping rough.[3] Drunkenness offences contrary to the Licensing Acts afford another example.[4] A third category comprises nuisance offences with a sexual element such as exposing the person, exhibiting indecent prints, and soliciting by prostitutes. The diversity of the Vagrancy Act 1824 is further illustrated by the existence of sundry offences such as being armed with an offensive weapon with intent to commit an arrestable offence, which cut across almost all categories of crime.[5] Many of these offences are in fact obsolete and have been replaced in practice by more modern enactments. A Home Office working party has recommended a number for repeal.

The penalty structure of the Vagrancy Act 1824 is archaic. A person who commits any of the offences specified in the Act is deemed to be a rogue and vagabond and is liable on summary conviction to imprisonment for a maximum period of three months or to a fine not exceeding £100. Recidivism results in the person being deemed to be an incorrigible rogue. A person may also be deemed an incorrigible rogue if he violently resists arrest as a rogue and vagabond by a constable and is subsequently convicted of the offence for which he or she was apprehended or if he breaks out of a place of legal confinement. Such a person may be committed in custody or on bail to the Crown Court for sentence.[6] The Crown Court may, if it thinks fit, order that the offender be imprisoned for a term not exceeding one year from the date of the order.[7] In appropriate circumstances, that is where the requirements of section 60 of the Mental Health Act 1959 are satisfied, the court may make a hospital order.[8] It may decide to make no order at all.[9] The court must,

---

3 Vagrancy Act 1824, s.4.
4 Licensing Act 1872, s.12; Licensing Act 1902, s.l. The matter is also covered by sundry local enactments.
5 Vagrancy Act 1824, s.8.
6 Vagrancy Act 1824, s.5; Criminal Justice Act 1948, s.83 (3) Sch.10; Criminal Justice Act 1967, s.103, Sch.6; Magistrates Courts Act 1971, s.56(1).
7 See further for details, 11 "Halsbury's Laws of England" (4th edn. 1976), p. 611.
8 These could be quite restrictive. The section requires that certain medical criteria be met and that arrangements have been made for the person's admission into hospital. See further, C. F. Shoolbred "A Guide to Recent Criminal Legislation" (1968) pp. 29–35.
9 *R.* v. *Jackson* [1974] 1 Q.B. 517.

if it proceeds to sentence, sentence the offender as an incorrigible rogue and not for the offence for which he was convicted.[10] Because the term "incorrigible rogue" denotes a status rather than an offence, the court cannot suspend a sentence of imprisonment passed upon a person as an incorrigible rogue,[11] nor make a probation order, an impediment thought by one court to be deplorable.[12]

The Vagrancy Acts and Itinerants

We begin by considering the vagrancy laws in their relation to homeless persons. A concatenation of offences and police powers applies. None of these offences is directed towards poverty as such. Each appears to describe particular behaviour. It is important to know what offences and police powers in aid apply. It is interesting to know in what circumstances certain powers will be used and others, apparently applicable, ignored.

Section 4 of the Vagrancy Act 1824 declares a rogue and vagabond to be any person wandering abroad and lodging in any barn or outhouse or in any deserted or unoccupied building, or in the open air, or in any tent or waggon and not giving a good account of himself or herself. The Vagrancy Act 1935 requires proof either that the person on the occasion in question was directed to a reasonably accessible place of shelter where accommodation is provided free of charge and has failed to apply for or been refused accommodation there, or is a person who regularly wanders abroad and notwithstanding the availability of shelter lodges or attempts to lodge in a manner forbidden by the section, or that by or in the course of such lodging he causes or appears likely to cause damage to property, infection with vermin, or other offensive consequence. The limitations were inserted in the law to ensure that a person who sleeps out from necessity is not to be treated as a criminal (Brown, 1936). Even before the 1935 Act it was police policy not to charge under s.4 unless there were grounds for thinking that the person concerned was of bad character or was found in circumstances likely to cause danger or nuisance to the community (Anon., 1933).

The offence of sleeping rough is today seldom charged. It is largely a metropolitan problem. According to a recent Home Office Report (1974, p. 6) figures for the years 1970–1972 disclose these conviction rates: 1970 = 394, 1971 = 401, 1972 = 373. In 1970 the figure for Metropolitan London was 155 persons and in 1971 it was 175 persons (comprising 150 men and 25 women) (Commissioner of Police, 1971, p. 51). No figures appear in the Re-

---

10   *R. v. Walters* [1969] 1 Q.B. 255.
11   *R. v. Graves* [1976] 4 C.L. 266.
12   *R. v. Jackson, supra.*

port of the Commissioner of Police for the Metropolis for 1972, but the figures above indicate that about half the offences dealt with were committed in London. These low enforcement figures can be explained on several grounds. In part they are due to a degree of police tolerance of persons who, while sleeping out, are neither alcoholics nor visible public nuisances. The police often ignore men who conceal themselves from public view. Derelict buildings provide a relatively safe haven although the Act applies to them (Archard 1975, p. 62). In part the low figures are attributable to the inhibiting requirement on the police first to direct a person found sleeping out to a free and readily available shelter. There is a shortage of these. Central London is badly served in this respect. In part offences which perhaps could be dealt with under the Vagrancy Acts are dealt with under the Licensing Acts. In part also, persons found sleeping on the roadways or pavements may be moved on or arrested for obstruction of highways or footpaths, provisions sometimes overlooked by persons who complain of unlawful police activity. There is no shortage of police powers.[13] In addition to these considerations, there is a reluctance to arrest persons who will often be socially inadequate or mentally disturbed.

The Home Office Working Party has suggested changes to the offence of sleeping rough, the effect of which may well be to increase the use of this offence. The Working Party notes that the substitution of casual wards by reception centres (and, they might have noted, the decline in other forms of accommodation such as the common-lodging house) has meant that the assumption of a general availability of free accommodation made in the Vagrancy Acts is no longer realistic, and accommodation is grouped in a relatively few areas. The police are thus inhibited in the enforcement of the offence. It was also felt that the offence failed adequately to provide for those who, by sleeping out, created a nuisance. The problem is admittedly, even in law enforcement terms, marginal. Thus the Working Party notes that mentally disordered persons can be dealt with under the powers contained in s.136 of the Mental Health Act 1959. Young people under 17 who become vagrant can be dealt with under the Children and Young Persons Acts. Itinerants who might molest wayfarers or who loiter near dwellings with intent to steal can be dealt with under other Vagrancy Act offences dealing with enclosed premises or as suspected persons, of which more hereafter, or under the burglary provisions of the Theft Act 1968. Persons refusing to maintain themselves may be dealt with under s.25 of the Supplementary Benefits Act 1976 for wilfully failing to maintain themselves (Home Office, 1974, para. 32).

Nonetheless, in order to cope with this residual problem of verminous

---

[13]   See Licensing Act 1872, s.12; Criminal Justice Act 1967, s.91(1) and (4) discussed *post* as to drunken persons, and s.121 of the Highways Act 1959 as to obstruction of the highway generally.

tramps who settle down in the hallways of flats or sleep in pedestrian subways or shop doorways, or of hippie vagrants who detract from the amenities of seaside resorts, the Home Office Working Party suggests an offence of
sleeping rough and causing a nuisance by doing so. The offence is not to
cover squatting. It is proposed to exclude cases in which persons have entered
into settled occupation of a dwelling house (Home Office, 1974, para. 33).
Despite protests by such groups as the Howard League who regard imprisonment as a bad answer to the problems posed by vagrants and alcoholics, the
Working Party remains persuaded of the desirability of such an offence
(Howard League for Penal Reform, 1975). It rejected suggestions that
the offence be restricted to the despoliation of property or refusing to leave
property as soon as reasonably possible after being ordered to leave by a
person entitled to occupation (Home Office, 1976, para. 3). The real need as
seen by the Working Party is to ensure adequate police powers against persons who sleep rough in places like seaside resorts and who cause a nuisance
by doing so. Here as elsewhere there appears to be an inference that no
action will be taken unless commercial interests are touched. Arrest and
prosecution will be a last resort. The police will try to induce the person to go
to a shelter or at least to find a place for the night where his presence will not
be offensive. In effect, this takes us back, in some measure, to the situation
as it existed before 1935. It seems apparent that the main thrust of the proposal, which the government has adopted, is against young persons whose
habits cause nuisance rather than against the small number of vagrants who
sleep rough, who cause a nuisance, and who cannot be dealt with under any
other provision. Arguably at least persons sleeping rough because they cannot find accommodation should not be made criminally liable for doing so.
One should perhaps recall that when persons sleeping rough were interviewed
for the National Assistance Board (1966, para. 407) some 24·5% gave lack
of accommodation as a reason. There are therefore some persons prepared
to ascribe sleeping rough to necessity. The proposed offence is of course cast
in terms of nuisance, but that, as a limitation, is not very impressive since a
court is likely to accept the conclusory evidence of a constable. In effect what
is proposed is to jettison a statutory defence based on necessity because
casual wards and other itinerant accommodation having been progressively
reduced, perhaps in a fit of reforming zeal, perhaps to release land for
development, the law can no longer be worked. The extent to which a common law defence of necessity could be raised is obscure. The accused's
perception may differ from the objective facts, viz., that supplementary benefit was available or that a centre was a "reasonable" distance away. What is
not yet clear, at any rate according to Lord Simon of Glaisdale in *Lynch* v.
Director of Public Prosecutions for Northern Ireland,[14] is whether necessity

---

14 [1975] A.C. 653 at p. 686.

is to be judged in subjective or objective terms. It would be unsatisfactory either to await litigation or the millennial prospect of a Criminal Code in which the matter would be dealt with.[15] It is, however, problematic whether homeless single persons will be much affected by the proposed changes. Certainly geriatric cases and some mentally disordered persons who are not so obviously deranged as automatically to be dealt with under the Mental Health Act 1959 might fall within its sweep. It is doubtful whether the proposal will have a much wider effect on homeless persons. We do not know how discretion will be exercised. Seaside resorts will be much easier to regulate on summer weekends. It is perhaps regrettable that a more limited proposal which would enable police powers to be exercised against persons sleeping rough or misconducting themselves in certain specified areas was not endorsed.

A more formidable scheme of controls stems from the Licensing Acts. These are of course not directed in terms towards homeless persons as such. They have, however, a considerable application to them. Section 91 of the Criminal Justice Act 1967 which has now been brought into force provides that any person who in any public place is guilty, while drunk, of any disorderly behaviour may be arrested without warrant by any person and shall be liable on summary conviction to a fine not exceeding £50.[16] Several former enactments which authorised imprisonment in cases of drunkenness are repealed.[17] The Home Office Report (1971, para. 3.8) points out that the measure will by itself remove only a small number of drunkenness offenders from local prisons since most are fined and ultimately imprisoned for non-payment of fines. Furthermore, imprisonment will still be available for aggravated offences other than drunk and disorderly such as drunk and indecent under s.29 of the Town Police Clauses Act 1847 or s.58 of the Metropolitan Police Act 1839. In addition, s.1 of the Licensing Act 1902, provides that if a person is found drunk in any highway or other public place, whether a building or not, or on any licensed premises, and appears to be incapable of taking care of himself, he may be apprehended and dealt with according to law. This last phrase refers to certain provisions of the Town Police Clauses Act 1847, the Metropolitan Police Act 1839 and the London Hackney Carriages Act 1835.

Police powers have already been modified by the discretionary provisions

---

15 The Law Commission Working Paper No. 65, *Defences of General Application* paras. 41–42 recommended that the defence be phrased subjectively.
16 Brought into effect by Criminal Justice Act 1967 (Commencement No. 4) Order, 1977. S.I. 1977/2139, and for details H.O. Circular No. 3/78. Note that sub-s.5 of the Act was repealed by s.91(2) and Sch. 7 of the Criminal Law Act 1977 (section not to be brought into force until Secretary of State satisfied that sufficient care and treatment facilities are available).
17 e.g. Metropolitan Police Act 1839; City of London Police Act 1839, s.27; Town Police Clauses Act 1847, s.29.

of s.34 of the Criminal Justice Act 1972 which provides that where a constable has a power of arrest under the statutes mentioned above, he may, if he thinks fit, take him to any place approved by the Home Secretary as a medical treatment centre for alcoholics.[18] A person taken to such a centre is not liable to be detained there, but he may be charged with an offence. At present only two centres have been established on an experimental and temporary basis.

The offences created by these statutes, and the police powers which they attract apply only in respect of conduct in a public place which is defined in s.8 of the Licensing Act 1902 to include any place to which the public have access whether on payment or otherwise. The term therefore would cover parks, railway platforms,[19] and places of public resort but not private houses. Under s.91 of the Criminal Justice Act 1967, it also includes any highway and any premises or place to which the public have or are permitted to have access whether on payment or otherwise. Private houses and even derelict buildings are not included, but the police can in such cases resort to s.4 of the Vagrancy Act 1824.

Powers of arrest under these sections apply where the person concerned is apparently drunk; where the circumstances are such as to warrant an honest belief upon reasonable grounds that the offence is being committed by the person arrested.[20]

Not surprisingly, there is little authority on the construction of these enactments, at any rate outside the area of motor vehicle law with which we are not at this point concerned. The courts have been content to hold that whether a person is drunk or not is a question of fact; that is, a person is drunk whom an ordinary reasonable person would consider to be so.[21]

The Licensing Acts are of course commonly invoked. Tables 1 and 2, taken respectively from the Reports of H.M. Inspector of Constabulary and the Commissioner of Police for the Metropolis, covering the years 1971–1977, disclose the extent to which the Licensing Act provisions are employed.

These figures of course provide no more than a rough impression. Table 1 records convictions and Table 2 records persons proceeded against, not all of whom are eventually convicted. Thus, in 1977 in metropolitan London, of the 44,139 persons proceeded against, 37,419 were convicted. In addition 808 persons proceeded against for other offences were also charged with drunkenness and 686 were convicted (Commissioner of Police 1977). It seems

---

[18] Brought into force by Criminal Justice Act 1972 (Commencement No. 5) Order 1976 No. 299.

[19] *Re Davis* (1857) 2 H. & N. 149.

[20] *Trebeck* v. *Croudace* [1918] 1 K.B. 158; *Barnard* v. *Gorman* [1941] A.C. 378 at pp. 394–395 *per* Lord Wright.

[21] *R.* v. *Presdee* (1927) 20 Cr.App.R. 95.

Table 1. *Convictions for drunkenness and drunkenness with aggravation in England and Wales (including metropolitan London).*

Year	Drunkenness	Drunkenness with aggravation
1977	49,483	53,746
1976	50,592	49,483
1975	49,239	50,400
1974	49,963	47,894
1973	51,453	45,326
1972	47,348	40,888
1971	43,681	39,280

a pity that police statistics are not presented on a uniform basis. Another difficulty is that the figures are undifferentiated; they apply to all arrests and proceedings for drunkenness whatever the circumstances of the offender and the offence. A number of cases therefore do not apply to homeless single persons, but it is known that vagrant alcoholics account for a sizeable proportion of the total figure. The Home Office Report (1971, Appendices H and J) finds that habitual offenders are generally middle-aged. Findings by Gath (1968) are similar. He set out to examine the characteristics of male drunkenness offenders before London courts. His study discloses a concentration of offenders in the age ranges 36–45 and 46–55. In the courts studied these age groups accounted for 55% of offenders. Of all the offenders in his sample, 50% had been arrested at least once during the previous 12 months, and 30% had been arrested three or more times.

There is general agreement that arrest and imprisonment produce no lasting good to the vast majority of vagrant alcoholics. Why then are the Licensing Acts enforced by arrest and imprisonment, under what circum-

Table 2. *Persons proceeded against for simple drunkenness or drunkenness with aggravation, and the proportion per 1000 of the estimated population (metropolitan London).*

Year	Number of persons proceeded against	Estimated population	No. of persons proceeded against per 1000 of population
1977	44,139	7,446,000	5·9
1976	43,743	7,509,000	5·8
1975	40,583	7,597,000	5·3
1974	41,193	7,647,000	5·4
1973	45,107	7,764,280	5·8
1972	44,203	7,840,340	5·6
1971	42,098	7,902,904	5·3

stances do the police use their powers, and why are not other powers used? The answer seems to be that the rehabilitative ideal is easier to state than to attain. Vagrant alcoholics pose a public nuisance especially in the inner London boroughs. The police are therefore, in some measure, obliged to break up and disperse skid-row men from public places where they are begging, sleeping rough, or hanging around. Handling drunks is a distasteful activity for the police. Arrest involves onerous obligations. Concentration on drunks distracts police manpower from use against more serious crime. When a person has been arrested as drunk the station officer notes the symptoms of any apparent disorder. He must send for a police surgeon in order to ascertain whether the prisoner is suitable for detention in cells. If the surgeon rules that the man is unfit to be detained, he is sent to hospital. The hospital may or may not discharge him. If discharged, the man is usually arrested on a drunkenness charge, but in that case the surgeon may be called for a further certificate. If the man is held in cells he must be watched in order to ensure that he does not choke on vomit.[22]

As a result, the police employ a wide measure of discretion (Archard, 1975, p. 62 *et seq.*). A person will be arrested where he appears to be a danger to himself, or where there has been a complaint from the public about open spaces being occupied by vagrant alcoholics. The police will generally not intervene when a man is booked into a lodging house. In some cases non-intervention appears positively bizarre. Thus a complaint by park-keepers that they had seen policemen and ambulance drivers arguing as to who should take away a drunk with the result that neither did, leaving the park-keeper to cope with the situation (Cook, 1975, p. 44). On the other hand, vagrant alcoholics, from time to time, fall victim to a police mopping-up operation, and complain of harassment and of improper use by the police of the offence of suspected person loitering with intent under s.4 of the Vagrancy Act 1824 (Archard, 1975, p. 50).

The short-term imprisonment of vagrant alcoholics is occasionally justified as a means of putting men in contact with the social services, and even as a means of prolonging the life of vagrants, if only for a short period as the pattern is one of relapse into drinking upon release from prison. The dreary parade of alcoholics through the magistrates' courts continues. Archard (1975, pp. 86–87) concludes that prison is not a place where serious rehabilitation can be attempted. The alcoholic is imprisoned with other alcoholics. Such persons do not discuss the possibility of sobriety on release with their drinking mates. There is a general feeling of pessimism. It is seen essentially as a life denying process. Similarly, hospital treatment has helped very little as they are unwilling to accept vagrant alcoholics. Those which are

---

[22] I am indebted to officers of the Metropolitan Police for information. On the occasions for arrest see also Home Office [1971] para. 6.13.

sympathetic to alcoholics mainly admit alcoholics with some chance of recovery and have little wish to have beds occupied by skid-row alcoholics with nowhere to go on discharge (Cook, 1975, p. 7). Stewart (1975, pp. 29–30) notes that the alcoholic treatment units at three hospitals in Liverpool, Chester and Manchester are loath to take vagrant alcoholics. Admission is in any event via a general practitioner's certificate and most homeless single persons are not registered with a medical practice.

Hospital attitudes also affect the police in their use of powers under s.136 of the Mental Health Act 1959. Under s.136 (1) of the Mental Health Act 1959 a constable may remove a mentally disordered person whom he finds in a public place and who appears to him to be in immediate need of care and control to a place of safety. A police station is considered to be such a place, so is a hospital. The section thus affords a facility for securing the admission of a person to a mental hospital without medical intervention. The hospital must, however, be willing to receive him. The person can be kept there for not more than 72 hours for examination and for arrangements for admission for care and treatment. He may if necessary be kept in hospital compulsorily thereafter. Very few patients are admitted under this provision. Walker (1970, p. 265) estimates the figure at one in 200 patients, although there are no reliable statistics. There are a number of reasons for this. As the Butler Committee (1975, para. 9.4) noted, the statistics appear to show that s.136 powers are used frequently by the Metropolitan police but very little outside London. Thus Gostin (1976, p. 31) citing statistics emanating from the Department of Health and Social Security, concludes that admissions under s.136 in 1973 vary from 34 per 1000 in the South-West Metropolitan region, with an average for the Metropolitan region of 21 per 1000, to less than one in every 1000 persons admitted in Leeds, Sheffield and Manchester. From this he concludes that the Metropolitan Police abuse their powers under s.136. The conclusion certainly does not follow from the premise, but the premise itself appears, according to the Butler Committee (1975, paras. 9.4–9.6), to be misconceived. First, s.136 is only regarded as having been employed where the police themselves take the person somewhere. If the police or a bystander simply telephones for an ambulance, the admission to hospital will be recorded as a normal admission to hospital, probably under s.29 of the Mental Health Act 1959, as an admission for observation. In some forces standing orders dictate that a mentally disordered person wandering at large be dealt with in this way. Furthermore, the section is invoked when a person is taken to a police station as a place of safety. Some forces however appear to have assumed that the section applies only when persons are taken to hospital. This must have affected the statistical data available to researchers. The Department of Health and Social Security (1976, paras. 2.22–2.27) certainly concludes that s.136 is employed nationally and that police powers are in general not abused. Other relevant considerations can also be suggested.

The powers apply only where the person is found in a public place.[23] If he is on private premises the constable will call the person's general practitioner who will make any further necessary arrangements with the local authority's mental welfare officer. The patient will then not be shown as having been admitted pursuant to police intervention. In the case of persons found in a public place, the police will intervene, usually on request from a member of the public, but only in clear cases. Eccentricity is not a ground for intervention. Typical cases are those where a person is a danger to himself or others or accosting people, or behaving in an obscene fashion.[24] Such arrests impose onerous obligations on the police. They must negotiate with a hospital in order to secure admission. In Metropolitan London standing arrangements exist, fortunately, for the admission to hospital of s.136 cases. In other areas, apparently, arrangements need to be worked out.[25] In cases of difficulty admission will be negotiated by the police surgeon. The patient will, ultimately, be delivered to the hospital in the appropriate catchment area. Admission may, as we have noted, be shown as occurring under other provisions such as the emergency procedure under s.29. The patient may well not remain in hospital. Many chronically ill persons go in and out of hospital through a revolving door. Rollin (1969, p. 42) found that 23 % of discharged patients are generally incapable of surviving unaided outside hospital for as long as a week. It is therefore not surprising that the police are not astute to discover cases of mental illness in the vagrant population. The police are aware of the attitude of hospitals and of the difficulty, if not impossibility, of doing anything for vagrant alcoholics.

There is no doubt that there is a substantial degree of mental illness among persons arrested under the Licensing Acts and the Vagrancy Acts. Thus Rollin (1969, p. 86) notes that a number of persons arrested as "suspected persons" or "found on enclosed premises" are schizophrenics with substantial records, some for crimes of violence. Similarly sexual exhibitionism may be a symptom of depression (Henderson and Gillespie, 1969). In these cases, however, the power of disposition, committal to a hospital under the Mental Health Act 1959, or the making of a psychiatric probation order is in the hands of the court and the powers have no specific relation to vagrant persons (Cross, 1975, pp. 61–66).

A further matter requires mention. We have noted that a constable now has

---

23 Information obtained from officers of the Metropolitan Police and from Dr Richard Farmer, Department of Social Medicine, Western Hospital. On the inability of the police to arrest in a private dwelling under these powers, see *Carter* v. *Metropolitan Police Commissioner* [1975] 1 W.L.R. 507.

24 I am again indebted to Dr Richard Farmer and to the Metropolitan Police for information. See also Rollin (1969).

25 Thus in Greater London a place of safety is generally to be a hospital and the four Thames Regional Health Authorities have been asked to designate hospitals for the purpose. See Department of Health and Social Security, *op.cit.* at n.61 *supra*, para. 2.27.

a discretionary power to take an arrested person to a detoxification centre. Such centres are therapeutic in essence. This response to the problem is in an experimental stage and it is too early to determine how well it will work. Cook (1975, pp. 107–113) warns against over-optimism on the part of the police. Their role will be crucial. He thus states:

> In England much of the pressure for the centres has come about because of dissatisfaction with the present legal system and its handling of the drunk. It is even worth pondering whether the (1971) Home Office Report itself would have been produced if prisons had not been so full and the drunks an obvious group that could be dealt with somewhere else. We need to separate our desire to reform the criminal justice system from the need to establish new treatment services for skid-row men. If this division is not clearly made, the result can be that we merely facilitate prevention of arrests by providing an alternative process to satisfy community interests which is in essence a system of "acceptable harassment". Arrests are outlawed and then relabelled.

There is therefore a need to instruct policemen concerning who is to go to such centres. If too many men are taken in, those who are conveniently available rather than the ill, if the centres as a result lose their medical emphasis, little good will be produced. A breakdown of relations between the police and the centre is a possibility. Furthermore, such centres should not be viewed as more than a very partial answer to the problem.

The Vagrancy Acts and Intending Criminals

There is a general agreement that many of the offences under the Vagrancy Act 1824 and related statutes are directed towards crime prevention as such. While sometimes used against homeless single persons they are in essence directed towards intending criminals (Home Office, 1976, para. 3; Moore, 1969). The two most prominent examples are "suspected person loitering with intent", a provision said to be much abused and of tyrannical scope (Rolph, 1964), and "being found in enclosed premises". Section 4 in which both these provisions are to be found is said to be directed to the protection of property and in particular, to the protection of goods awaiting transport from theft, and to protection from pickpockets in public places (O'Donoghue, 1964). It is certainly apt to apply to cases of petty pilfering in which vagrants are likely to be involved.

Among the persons who under s.4 may be deemed a rogue and vagabond and who under s.6 may be arrested without warrant are included:[26]

> . . . every suspected person or reputed thief, frequenting any river, canal, or navigable stream, dock, or basin, or any quay, wharf, or warehouse near or

---

[26]   Vagrancy Act 1824, s.4 as amended by Criminal Law Act 1967, Sch.2.

adjoining thereto, or any street, highway, or avenue leading thereto, or any place of public resort or any avenue leading thereto, or any street or any highway or any place adjacent to a street or highway with intent to commit an arrestable offence . . .

There is a similar power under s.64 of the Metropolitan Police Act 1839 which enables a constable to arrest without warrant all loose, idle and disorderly persons whom he shall find disturbing the public peace or whom he shall have good cause to suspect of having committed or being about to commit an offence. The section proceeds to deal with lying or loitering and in that connection is dealt with below. In addition there are powers under s.7 of the Metropolitan Police Act 1829, and s.193 of the Municipal Corporations Act 1882 which, as amended, authorise the arrest of idle and disorderly persons whom the constable finds to be disturbing the public peace.[27] The s.4 offence must be understood against the background of s.13 of the Prevention of Crimes Act 1871 which provides that in proving intent it shall not be necessary to prove that the person suspected was guilty of any particular act or acts tending to show intent but can be convicted from the circumstances taken with his known record. This is certainly severe.

Space precludes an extended treatment of all aspects of this offence (see Leigh, 1975a). Some matters, however, deserve mention. The person must, in order to be arrested and convicted, be a suspected person or reputed thief. He must be loitering with intent to commit an arrestable offence. He must be loitering in one of the places specified in the statute. The principal safeguard against abuse of police powers is the requirement that the person has acquired the status of reputed thief or fallen into the category of suspected thief before the commission of the acts or class of acts which led to his arrest. All that is required is that the accused be shown to have committed acts, before the arrest, of a kind apt to provoke suspicion.[28] The act which engendered suspicion and the act which led to arrest need not be separated by any particular or extended period of time.[29] The acts may be of the same class, e.g. trying car doors. Thus in *Cosh* v. *Isherwood*[30] which, incidentally, illustrates the artificiality of trying to separate the acts relied on to establish that the accused fell within the class of suspected person from those which led to arrest, the acts were of trying car doors. The accused having tried a number

---

[27] Municipal Corporations Act 1882, s.193 as amended by Criminal Law Act 1967, Sch. iii, Pt.iii.

[28] *Rawlings* v. *Smith* [1938] 1 K.B. 675; approving *Hartley* v. *Ellnor* (1917) 117 L.T. 304 and explaining *Ledwith* v. *Roberts* [1937] 1 K.B. 232; see further *Nakhla* v. *R.* [1975] 1 N.Z.L.R. 393 (P.C.) where the English authorities are collected and discussed. The term does not apply to persons of generally suspicious character; cf. *Cowles* v. *Dunbar* (1837) Mood. & M.37.

[29] *Pyburn* v. *Hudson* [1950] 1 All E.R. 1006.

[30] [1968] 1 All E.R. 383.

of car doors was approached by two observers who saw him doing so and left their car to approach him. His acts were said to be separated into those done before the observers left their car and those done after, yet it is hard to see how the actions of the observers could divide up the accused's conduct. In *Fitzgerald* v. *Lyle* a conviction was supported even though the accused was seen to try only two vehicle doors one after the other.[31] This illustrates that the suspected person clause is a weak protection against harassment. Furthermore, "suspected person" and "reputed thief" are not synonymous. A person may be a suspected person on a given day even though he has not been previously convicted.[32] Conversely, and this may be the explanation of *Fitzgerald* v. *Lyle* where the accused was known by the arresting constable to be on bail, a person could be a reputed thief without being a suspected person. In any such case s.13 of the Prevention of Crimes Act 1871 could be a mighty engine of oppression indeed. Furthermore, it appears that constables are entitled to rely on an accused's previous convictions as bringing him within the category of reputed thief and therefore arrestable even though they are unaware of his record at the time of arrest.[33]

The accused must be loitering. This does not mean simply standing or waiting in the street but means loitering in such a way as to indicate that the person was idling in the street for some unlawful purpose.[34] But few decisions interpret this concept restrictively.[35] To some extent it seems that these concepts feed on each other. Thus one finds it stated that frequenting means being in a given place for long enough to effect a criminal purpose (Anon, 1954).

A Home Office Working Party recommends the retention and modernisation of this offence (Home Office, 1974, 1976; Leigh, 1975b). They identify a need to protect the public from someone who is apparently embarking on a criminal enterprise. The would-be pickpocket in a crowd is an obvious example. The new "suspected person" offence would be limited to the case of a person whose antecedent conduct in a public place reveals his intention to commit an arrestable offence. The reputed thief limb would go. Whether the person's record if known can be taken together with his conduct to render him a suspected person is not clearly stated, but there seems little reason why it should not be relied on to give colour to the person's acts. Whether the provisions of s.13 of the Prevention of Crimes Act 1871 are to continue to apply is not stated. Much of the effect of the present s.4 may in fact derive from its availability since otherwise one might in practice be restricted to acts

---

31 [1972] Crim. L.R. 125.
32 *Hartley* v. *Ellnor* [1917] 117 L.T. 304.
33 *R.* v. *Clarke* [1950] 1 K.B. 523; cf. *R.* v. *Fairbairn* [1949] 2 K.B. 690.
34 *Ledwith* v. *Roberts* [1937] 1 K.B. 232; *Nakhla* v. *R.* [1975] 1 N.Z.L.R. 393 (P.C.); one can loiter in a motor car, see *Bridge* v. *Campbell* [1947] L.T. 444.
35 *Ledwith* v. *Roberts, supra*, is a rare example.

which approach the degree of proximity required for an attempt.[36] It will be of interest to see how far the government will restrict the offence. These finer points are unlikely however to impede the police much and the "suspected person" clause is in any event of peripheral significance in terms of convictions (Leigh, 1975b).

The other principal clause of s.4 deems to be a rogue and vagabond: ". . . every person being found in or upon any dwelling house, warehouse, coach-house, stable, or outhouse, or in any inclosed yard, garden or area, for any unlawful purpose . . ." This section is sometimes, it would seem, applied against vagrants (Archard, 1975, p. 50). If so the practice would amount to an abuse of powers since the courts have held that the "unlawful purpose" which the section requires must be to commit some definite criminal offence.[37] Just what powers the police do exercise to move persons on from derelict buildings where there is no element of lodging is obscure. In metropolitan London the police may be able to rely on s.64 of the Metropolitan Police Act 1837 which enables a constable to arrest, *inter alia*: ". . . all persons whom he shall find between sunset and the hour of eight in the morning lying or loitering in any highway, yard, or other place, and not giving a satisfactory account of themselves". On the other hand, while the section is not restricted textually to apprehended criminal conduct, it does not apply in terms to houses or other buildings and a construction *ejusdem generis* suggests that it is not meant to. There is of course the further possibility that in some cases the police may be able to move persons on, acting as the agent of the occupier. It seems probable, however, that the ambiguities of the offence of obstruction of a constable suffice for the most part. Vagrants, whether alcoholic or otherwise, are unlikely to vindicate their rights before the magistrates.

Once again, the Home Office Working Party recommends retention of the offence notwithstanding that most cases which before 1968 were charged as vagrancy are now charged as burglary.[38] The essence of the new offence would be trespassory entry into a place where goods are stored. The person would be guilty of an offence if he were unable to give a satisfactory account of his presence. In effect, he would be under a duty to raise the issue that he was present for a lawful purpose before that issue became a live one; this is truly draconian. It becomes even more so if s.13 of the Prevention of Crimes

---

[36] On the notion of proximate act in attempt, see J. C. Smith and B. Hogan, "Criminal Law" (3rd ed. 1974), pp. 194–198.

[37] *Hayes* v. *Stevenson* [1860] 3 L.T. 296.

[38] Theft Act 1968, s.9 defines burglary as entry of a building as a trespasser with intent to commit theft, inflicting grievous bodily harm, rape, and unlawful damage to the building or anything in it, or if a person has entered simply as a trespasser without a criminal intent, he steals or attempts to steal or inflicts or attempts to inflict grievous bodily harm on anyone in it.

Act 1871 continues to apply. The offence is thought necessary to deal with cases where there is no evidence of specific criminal intent but there are strong indications from the very presence of the accused that such intent is present. It is, they suggest, difficult to see how much farther the Theft Act 1968 or the law of attempt could be pushed in such circumstances. There is, with respect, some question whether any offence should apply. But will the new crime apply to homeless persons? The Home Office Working Party concludes that it will not; the offence is not directed at homeless persons. If, however, such persons are found on premises in suspicious circumstances, it is reasonable to ask them for an explanation (Home Office, 1974, para. 60). In relation to homeless persons this is no doubt correct, the balance of power will not be altered particularly.[39] The balance is more likely to shift as a result of the Law Commission's proposals to create an offence of remaining on residential premises to deal with the problem of squatting. These proposals, embodied in the Criminal Law Act 1977, create offences of using or threatening violence to secure entry to premises on which there is another person who opposes entry, and of greater importance for the purposes of this paper, make it an offence for a person who trespasses to fail to leave premises when required to do so by a displaced residential occupier. An offence of impeding a sheriff's bailiff is created. This will put an obligation on the police to assist a dispossessed residential occupier.[40] Formerly, police assistance to dispossessed residential occupiers was given pursuant to force instructions (Lane, 1975). The Act also gives a power of entry and search for the purpose of exercising a power of arrest under these provisions.[41] This may facilitate the use of charges of criminal damage against squatters since the police, once lawfully on premises, will be able to note damage and to confiscate matter of evidentiary value.[42] Police practices may as a result change in such cases as these.[43] Many homeless single persons, if squatters, are not likely to displace residential occupiers or refuse to leave premises and will not be substantially affected by these changes in the law.

Other offences dealing with acquisitive crime need not detain us here, they are not in essence directed towards homeless single persons. Such matters as begging, fortune-telling and unlicensed peddling appear in the Vag-

---

[39] Because the offence requires that the person intend to commit a criminal offence it would not enable a constable to terminate a simple trespass.

[40] Criminal Law Act 1977, s. 6, 7 and 10; and see Law Commission Report No. 76, "Report on Conspiracy and Criminal Law Reform", paras. 2.1–2.94.

[41] Criminal Law Act 1977, s.11.

[42] *Ghani* v. *Jones* [1970] 1 Q.B. 693.

[43] Arguably the offence of forcible detainer always applied but the police were reluctant to invoke it as it was an offence requiring jury trial. See Law Commission "Working Paper No. 76", Draft Conspiracy and Criminal Law Reform Bill cl.8, 11 and 13 (power of entry to effect an arrest). On the Statutes of Forcible Entry, see Law Commission, Working Paper No. 54, "Offences of Entering and Remaining on Property," paras. 8–22.

rancy Act 1824. Of these only the begging offence has been thought to relate to homeless persons. Section 3 of the Vagrancy Act 1824 renders an idle and disorderly person and liable to imprisonment for one month: ". . . every person wandering abroad, or placing himself or herself in any public place, street, highway, court or passage to beg or gather alms, or causing or procuring or encouraging any child or children so to do . . ."

This provision is to some extent superseded by s.14 of the Children Act 1908 which makes it an offence to procure a child to beg in a public place and by s.4(1) of the Children and Young Persons Act 1933 which makes it an offence to allow a person under 16 to be used for begging. The onus lies upon a person in custody, charge or control of such a child who allows the child to be on a street, premises or place, to prove that he did not allow the child to be there for the purpose of begging. The Vagrancy Act offence always was of narrow import. It applied only to persons who adopted a particular habit and mode of life. In order to fall within it a person must adopt wandering abroad to beg as a life style. It thus did not apply to strikers who went from house to house soliciting assistance in cash and kind.[44] In order to stop up this loophole, the House to House Collections Act 1939 was passed imposing a licensing requirement for collections for charitable purposes.

The Home Office Working Party (1976, paras. 13–18) recommends the abolition of the Vagrancy Act offence and the substitution of an offence of persistent begging. The behaviour of some persons can be a nuisance and even frightening; the best response is, they conclude, to cast the offence in terms of persistence. The Working Party concludes against the argument put forward by some organisations, that such an offence would penalise conduct which is a symptom of deprivation and in any event does not constitute a serious nuisance to the person accosted. Not all beggars are, they conclude, deprived. Plainly, no special provision is being made for those who are. One can foresee enforcement problems, not least in proving persistence in cases where the beggar has not been kept under surveillance.

Persistently Failing to Support Oneself

Finally, we may note the offence under s.25 of the Supplementary Benefits Act 1976, which exists in order to inhibit persons from resorting unmeritoriously, to supplementary benefit or to the amenities of reception centres. The section provides that a person who persistently refuses or neglects to maintain himself and who is awarded benefit or free board and lodging in a reception centre commits an offence and is liable on summary

---

44 *Pointon* v. *Hill* [1884] 12 Q.B.D. 306.

conviction to imprisonment for a term not exceeding three months or to a fine not exceeding £100 or to both. A person is not deemed to refuse or neglect to maintain himself or any other person by reason only of anything done or omitted in furtherance of a trade dispute. Under the old vagrancy provision from which this section ultimately derives the courts held that a person could not commit the offence unless he were able to maintain himself when he began to obtain benefit.[45]

This sort of provision reflects the aim of the Supplementary Benefits Commission to make provision for people to adopt a more settled way of life. It is for this purpose that reception centres are provided (Anon, 1936; Cook, 1975, pp. 156–159). The theme is an old one. We find the Poor Law Board in 1848 seeking to distinguish between the vagrant and the reclaimable citizen by suggesting the use of a police officer as an assistant relieving officer. From time to time further measures were suggested to separate the obdurate from the rest (Glen, 1882)—none has worked. Stewart (1975, p. 60) records that for 1965, in respect of the section's precursors the last year for which statistics were routinely published, 22 men were convicted of using centres when capable of maintaining themselves, and a further 67 were prosecuted for breach of reception centre regulations. Current practice seems to be to admit men who follow an itinerant way of life with no known address or who appear to be starting a career of lodging house use. Current policy is to open more reception centres, subject to financial constraints. There is a policy of letting people stay, and to wait for some time, apparently three weeks, before pressing them to participate positively in the reception centre's programme, as by discussing their situation. The figures are shown in Table 3 in conjunction with the figures for convictions for breach of reception centre regulations which are consistent with the same policy.

Table 3. Convictions for using reception centres and also for breach of reception centre regulations. Source—Parl. Question and Answer, written answer Tuesday, October 19, 1976, H.C. Deb. 5th Series, Vol. 917, col. 385.

Year	Convictions for using reception centres	Convictions for breach of reception centre regulations
1965	22	67
1966	4	N/A
1967	0	56
1968	1	86
1969	0	80
1970	0	69
1971	1	35
1972	0	22
1973	0	31

[45] *St. Saviour's Union* v. *Burbridge* [1900] 2 Q.B. 695.

The lack of an address does not act as a bar to the receipt of supplementary benefit. That is available whether the person attends a reception centre or not, but the rate is very low. In general the under-use by vagrants and vagrant alcoholics of the supplementary benefit system is not attributable to the presence of punitive sanctions wielded by the Supplementary Benefits Commission or the Department of Health and Social Security. It reflects a dislike in dealing with certain offices, and general inadequacy.

Conclusion

This has been a rambling survey. Unhappily, perhaps, the law is diverse. It reflects, all too clearly, that the laws concerning vagrancy and vagrants were enacted at different times, as the result of diverse impulses and perceptions of social problems. They also reflect the inability of society to arrive at a set of solutions to the diverse problems of vagrancy, chronic alcoholism, and mental illness characteristic of many itinerants. Furthermore, the problems faced by homeless persons may well, as we find ourselves again in an era of recession, have been exacerbated by a shortage of accommodation caused by the well-intentioned closure of lodging houses and casual wards. To problems of this character the criminal law seems almost irrelevant. At best it keeps the streets clean. It may afford an occasion for taking someone to a detoxification centre or for suggesting other accommodation or for putting him in touch with the social services who may or may not be able to help. It cannot be thought of as an answer to the problem of vagrancy.

Acknowledgements

It is right to record a debt to colleagues and friends who have supplied criticism and information. In particular I should like to mention my colleagues, Professor J. A. G. Griffith and J. W. Carrier, Esq., Mrs Mary Ochs of the Camden Borough Council Social Welfare Department, and Sir John Langford-Holt, M.P.

References

Anon (1933). Sleeping out. *J.P.* **97**, 787.
Anon (1936). Vagrancy in Scotland. *J.P.* **100**, 618.
Anon (1954). Suspected persons. *Sol. J.* **98**, 431.

Archard, P. (1975). "The Bottle Won't Leave You." Alcoholics Recovery Project, London.
Brown, M. (1936). Vagrancy and sleeping out. *Can. Bar. Rev.* **14**, 442.
Butler Committee (1975). "Report of the Committee on Mentally Disordered Offenders", Cmnd 6244. HMSO, London.
Chambliss, W. (1969). The law of vagrancy. In "Crime and the Legal Process" (Chambliss, W., ed). Dryden Press, New York.
Commissioner of Police (1971). "Report for the Metropolis." HMSO, London.
Commissioner of Police (1975). "Report for the Metropolis." HMSO, London.
Cook, T. (1975). "Vagrant Alcoholics." Routledge and Kegan Paul, London.
Cross, R. (1975). "The English Sentencing System" 2nd edition. Butterworth, London.
Department of Health and Social Security (1976). "A Review of the Mental Health Act 1959." DHSS, London.
Gath, D. (1968). The male drunk in court. In "The Drunkenness Offence" (Cook, T., Gath, D. and Hensman, C., eds). Pergamon Press, Oxford.
Glen, W. C. (1882). "The Pauper Inmates Discharge and Regulation Act 1871." London.
Gostin, L. (1976). "A Human Condition", Mental Health Act from 1959 to 1975. MIND, London.
Henderson, D. K. and Gillespie, R. D. (1969). "Textbook of Psychiatry", 10th edition. Oxford University Press, Oxford.
Holdsworth, W. E. (1924). "History of English Law", Vol. IV. Sweet and Maxwell, London.
Holloway, J. (1970). "They Can't Fit In", Bedford Square Press, London.
Home Office (1971). "Habitual Drunken Offenders." HMSO, London.
Home Office (1974). "Working Paper of the Working Party on Vagrancy and Street Offences." HMSO, London.
Home Office (1976). "Report of the Working Party on Vagrancy and Street Offences." HMSO, London.
Howard League for Penal Reform (1975). "Whose Discretion?" Annual Report 1974–1975, London.
Lambert, J. (1869). "Vagrancy Laws and Vagrants." London.
Lane, E. O. (1975). Letter to *The Times*, 18 August.
Langbein, J. (1976). The historical origins of the sanction of imprisonment for serious crime. *J. Leg. Stud.* **5**, 35.
Leigh, L. H. (1975a). "Police Powers in England and Wales." Butterworth, London.
Leigh, L. H. (1975b). Vagrancy, morality and decency. *Crim. Law Rev.* **1975**, 381.
McWilliams, W. (1975). Homeless offenders in Liverpool. In "Some Male Offender Problems", Home Office Research Studies No. 20. HMSO, London.
Moore, B. (1969). Vagrancy and related offences. *Harv. Civil Rights Law Rev.* **4**, 291.
National Assistance Board (1966). "Homeless Single Persons." HMSO, London.
O'Donoghue, F. (1964). Loiterers, vagrants and law reformers, *Sol. J.* **108**, 95.
Rolph, C. H. (1964). Criminal law. In "Law Reform Now" (Gardiner, G. and Martin, A., eds). Gollancz, London.
Rollin, H. (1969). "The Mentally Disordered Offender and the Law." Pergamon Press, Oxford.
Sackville, R. (1976). "Homeless People and the Law." Australian Government Commission of Inquiry into Poverty, Canberra.
Sherry, A. H. (1960). Vagrants, rogues and vagabonds—old concepts in need of revision. *Cal. L. Rev.* **48**, 557.

Stewart, J. (1975). "Of No Fixed Abode: Vagrancy and the Welfare State." Manchester University Press, Manchester.

Walker, N. (1970). "Crime and Punishment in Britain." Edinburgh University Press, Edinburgh.

Campaigning for the Homeless and Rootless

NICHOLAS BEACOCK

Improvements in the position of minorities in society almost always happen in small steps. A slight change in the small print of Government policy or a successful local initiative can often lead to significant changes in the status and conditions of the weak and the poor. The task of a campaign on behalf of single homeless people is to pursue those small steps which seem likely to make daily life more tolerable and just for men and women who may have known only homelessness for years. The temptation is to fight the battles of the past or to nail one's colours exclusively to blueprints for the future.

The struggle to secure for the single homeless poor the right to share the opportunities and services open to the majority of their fellow citizens in Britain in the last quarter of the twentieth century, is of course hampered by the effects of images and attitudes, policies and provisions inherited from long ago and perpetuated today. Although the past two decades have seen a flurry of activity, publicity, studies and recommendations by statutory and voluntary agencies, the living conditions of those single poor people who become homeless or who can expect no better, and often much worse shelter, than a temporary bed in a lodging house would make George Orwell feel quite at home were he to return on his legendary circuit. What is more, the attack on attitudes which have in the past caused the single homeless poor to be written off is currently made difficult by the visible trend towards a "boot-strings" philosophy as the decline in Britain's economy is felt by wide sections of the community.

The struggle is made doubly difficult in that recent activity on behalf of the single homeless poor has, to a large extent, reflected the fact that single people generally have become subject to increasingly acute housing problems. The

119

rise of more organised and disciplined squatting movements, and the growing awareness of the Department of the Environment of the housing needs of single people are primarily responses to the decline in accommodation available in the private rented sector, which has traditionally been assumed to be able to cater for single people. In this situation it is highly probable that single homeless poor people, particularly those categorised as vagrants, will be afforded low priority in competition with the needs of single people with modest incomes.

Society's major response to the problems of its minorities has always been to decide that they, rather than the social system, are responsible for their plight. The history of provision for the single homeless poor shows a propensity to identify the homeless person as in some way inadequate, then to set up means of treating his alleged inadequacy. Great weight has been given to this approach by the use of the label "single homeless people" to define the needs of those individuals who become homeless and who live with homelessness for years.

Many will no doubt argue that the use of the words "single homeless people" to subsume the particular needs of the single homeless poor is at least an improvement on earlier, more pejorative labels attached to individuals caught in the web of homelessness. It enables, they will say, the debate about meeting their needs to be conducted by social policy makers whereas earlier labels left homeless individuals firmly at the mercy of punitive or redemptive approaches. The vocabulary may have changed, but the status and condition of the single homeless poor has changed little.

In this chapter, I shall first set out the primary causes of homelessness among single poor people. I shall then seek to show that current Government policy, far from attacking these ordinary causes, serves to reinforce the disadvantaged position of single poor people who become homeless. In conclusion I shall outline the steps forward which seem most likely to improve the chances of single homeless poor people.

Primary Causes

One of the most common responses to homelessness is the view that the Welfare State has provided ample facilities for individuals to avoid the trap of destitution and vagrancy. Those now in that position must be there by choice. Confirmation of this response is to be found in a recent comparative study of images of poverty in the member-states of the European Economic Community (Commission of the European Communities, 1977). Respondents in each of the nine EEC countries were asked how much they thought their public authorities do for the poor. Of the sample of opinion taken from the United Kingdom, 20% thought that British authorities do "too much" to combat poverty (compared with 2% in France and Italy), while 35% thought that the authorities do "about what they should" (compared with 12% in Italy and 23% in France). Yet even a cursory look at the position of single poor people in terms of housing and income-maintenance shows what little choice individuals can exercise given existing structural factors.

Housing

Since the first World War the general supply of housing has been influenced by two consistent public demands, the desire of people to own their own homes and the expectation of increased privacy and therefore less over-crowding. The single poor are largely excluded from benefiting from the results of these two demands.

In 1976, the proportion of the housing stock of some 18·1 million dwellings in England and Wales in owner-occupation amounted to 55% or about 10 million dwellings, a proportion which had increased from 31% in 1951. Yet in 1971, only 4% of these homes were owned by single people of working age (Department of Environment and Welsh Office, 1977). Over the same period, the private rented sector had shrunk from 52% of all dwellings in 1951 to only 15% in 1976, or 2·6 million dwellings, a relentless decline linked directly to the trends in general demand. In 1971, 35% of the furnished lettings within this sector were to single people of working age.

For those single people on low incomes, dependent traditionally on their ability to compete for tenancies in the private rented sector, these changes in the first two sectors of housing supply need not have been as serious as they have proved to be had the increasingly important public sector altered the patterns of its allocations in the last 25 years. By 1976, 30% of the housing stock was to be found in this sector, amounting to 5·5 million dwellings, compared with 17% in 1951. Yet in 1971, only 4% of all local authority tenants in England and Wales were single working people living alone. Only in the last two or three years have a few public housing authorities begun to adjust their building programmes to take account of the needs of single-person households, and many still have restrictions against registration for public housing by single people, while in the great majority the waiting-list system is such as to render registration little more than a token.

Housing policy has largely ignored the cumulative increase in the number of single-person households in the country, especially in inner-city areas, and the fact that these households have a desire to live as securely and independently as family households. Between 1961 and 1971 the total number of multi-person households in England and Wales increased by some 8% while the total number of one-person households increased by a staggering 86%. In 1971, there were some 3·3 million known one-person households of all ages, of which 1·3 million were men and women of working age, out of a total known household population of some 16·8 million.

Yet even these figures do not adequately cover concealed single-person households. There are at present about 8·5 million single people of working age in England and Wales, and there is a growing tendency for young single people to form their own separate households. In 1976, 275,000 individuals under 30 years old formed separate households, compared with 70,000 in 1961. Some indication of the housing conditions of many of these households can be gathered from the fact that in 1971, 86,000 unfurnished tenancies and 1·3 million furnished tenancies were being shared by these households; 52,000 of the unfurnished and 61,000 of the furnished tenancies were located in Greater London.

Greater London itself presents special stark problems for single people. A Greater London Council and London Boroughs Association study (1977b) reported as follows:

There are already a very sizeable number of one-person households in Greater London (646,000 of them) and an even larger number (968,000) of adults who were single, widowed or divorced but who were living in multi-person households in 1971. In addition, there were almost a quarter of a million (246,000) 16–19-year-olds living at home. Projections show no decrease in housing demand generally, and an increase absolutely and proportionately in one-person households. Much of this projected increase will come from rising expectations, for there is a growing tendency for single people currently sharing or living with parents to choose to live separately.

The emphasis of this last sentence is important, in that although the major increase in the number of single-person households in recent years has come from the elderly, rising expectations on the part of the young and of single people in middle age groups will without doubt affect future trends.

If the failure of supply to keep pace with demand has had serious consequences for single people generally, its effects on the prospects of unskilled single people living on the margins of homelessness have been disastrous. Increasing numbers of them have been forced to take refuge in accommodation in hostels, lodging houses and night shelters, in short in a form of accommodation incapable of providing the security or decency expected by the majority of the population. Worse still, this "communal" sector has itself experienced rapid decline in both the total number of establishments and the total number of beds available.

A Government survey of hostel and lodging-house accommodation used by single poor people, conducted in 1972 (Wingfield-Digby, 1976), showed an overall loss of beds nationally of some 17% since 1965 (from 37,845 beds to 31,253 beds). The only part of this provision to have increased its supply was that made by the small voluntary organisations, which had increased by some 16% to 4835 beds. Over the same period, private commercial establishments had lost 17% of their supply, while commercial hostels had lost 34%, usually as a result of the closure or upgrading of large establishments. We shall return to some of the implications of the changed ownership of this sector later.

Not only has this communal safety-net shelter for the single poor declined in quantity, it has also not improved in quality in line with the trends in conditions enjoyed by the majority of the population. The interim lodging house standards recommended by the Ministry of Housing to be applied to hostel accommodation specify the provision of one washbasin per five beds, one flush lavatory per eight beds and one bath per twelve beds, not very high standards by comparison with owner-occupied homes. Yet the 1972 survey already quoted found 51% of all hostel beds in places that fell below all three of these standards: 49% of the beds in establishments run by local authorities fell into this category. Altogether, 78% of the beds provided nationally were in places which fell below at least one of the three interim lodging house standards. Further, 85% of the establishments in the survey were in buildings erected before 1914.

Finally, some measure of the housing choice available to single poor people is indicated in that one in five of a sample of 2000 residents in the communal sector was a retirement pensioner. There can surely be no less fitting place to end one's days than a common-lodging house.

Income Maintenance

The recent period of very high unemployment has witnessed a return of that ancient British sport of scrounger-hunting, in which the consequences of the recession and of the dependence of increasing numbers of citizens, especially those without skills, on welfare benefits are visited on the claimants rather than the economic failure of the system. Our penchant for this game is again confirmed in the study of images of poverty within the EEC (Commission of European Communities, 1977). Respondents from each of the nine countries were asked to select the three most common causes of poverty from a list of nine possible causes. The aggregate of replies from the whole Community showed that a deprived childhood, lack of education and sickness/ill health were felt to be the most common causes. The UK sample, however, listed laziness, chronic unemployment and drink as the most common causes in Britain, lack of education being placed seventh, and a deprived childhood ninth and last.

Single people who become prone to homelessness are characterised by a

common lack of work skills and a high dependence on welfare benefits.
Although the 1972 Government survey of communal accommodation found
50 % of its sample interviewed to be working (a proportion which will without
doubt have declined by 1979 as a result of the recession), it drew attention to
the fact that the 50 % unemployment rate among this part of the population
compared with a national unemployment rate of 3·8 %. Further, the survey
showed that among the lodging-house population 26 % of residents were
semi-skilled, compared with 18 % of the national working population,
while 51 % were unskilled, compared with 8 % of the national working population (Wingfield-Digby, 1976).

In a report published to highlight the problems of this group, CHAR
(1976a) commented as follows:

> Unskilled manual jobs not only represent a small proportion of total jobs but
> one that is declining. The Department of Employment has shown that there
> was a net decline in unskilled and semi-skilled manual occupations between 1951
> and 1961, so that there were 170,000 fewer such jobs by 1961. It has been
> estimated that at one London Labour Exchange the ratio of vacancies for
> heavy labourers was never better than 1 to 35 and never above 1 to 155 for
> light labourers between 1968 and 1971. Since then the unemployment rate has
> doubled. Frank Field of Child Poverty Action Group has given some
> indication of what this means to those disadvantaged: "In September 1974
> the Department of Employment reported that for each vacancy for a general
> unskilled labourer they had 150 unemployed labourers on their books. By
> 1975 this ratio had risen to one vacancy for 9500 unemployed labourers"
> (*The Guardian*, 26 Jan. 1976).

Further weight to the problems facing the unskilled single poor is given in a
study of residents at the Camberwell Reception Centre (Tidmarsh and Wood,
1972) in which the authors state: "The fact that low-grade menial jobs and
casual work are the residents' main occupations hinders rather than helps
their 'resettlement' ".

Casual employment has traditionally formed a significant fall-back for
the unskilled poor. In July 1976, CHAR and the Low Pay Unit jointly
published a report on the position of casual employees seeking work in the
catering trade in London's West End through the Department of Employment's special employment exchange (Erlam and Brown, 1976). Despite the
fact that the ratio of applicants to vacancies was low, at that time up to 100
men and women were found to be willing to queue outside the office from
the early hours of the morning, and some through the night, for a job.
Catering workers are supposed to be protected by legal minimum wage rates
set by appointed Wages Councils and enforced by the Department of Employment's wages inspectorate. Catering Wages Councils have often set very
low minimum rates. For example, in July 1976 the minimum for a kitchen
porter in a licensed restaurant was only 65·2p per hour. Nevertheless, out of
24 workers interviewed who were covered by legal minima, the report found

18 to be receiving pay below the minimum rates. The report further found that these men had been directed to their jobs by the very same Department which had the duty to see that legal minima were enforced. Many workers were found to be earning between £2·50 and £4 per day, and the supply of vacancies was so intermittent as to make it likely that a casual job could only be obtained two or three days out of five. In April 1976, the New Earnings Survey estimated the average gross earnings of all full-time working men in the UK to be £71·80 per week, yet the CHAR/Low Pay Unit report found working men seeking casual employment earning less than one-fifth of this average.

In December CHAR (1976) conducted a further sample survey of the incomes of single homeless poor people, which was included in a submission to the Royal Commission on the Distribution of Incomes and Wealth. Thirty-four individuals who were interviewed at length provided information about their incomes. Their average income over the preceding week, including those of two people who were working, amounted to £10·92; 18 of the sample were in receipt of supplementary benefit, and on the basis of the current supplementary benefit rates, the survey calculated that seven of the 18 were receiving less than their entitlement.

The provision of benefits by the Supplementary Benefits Commission is supposed to form the respite against poverty for the poor. Far from providing the single homeless poor with an incentive to scrounge, let alone with the means to exercise choice, both the levels and the methods of administration applied to the single homeless poor leave wide areas of choice to the administrators of the scheme. Suffice it to say at this point that at the time when the CHAR/Low Pay Unit found casual employees enlisting at the special employment exchange to be likely to earn between £2·50 and £4 per day, the statutory daily payment for a claimant without a fixed address was £1·40.

Lodging house dwellers who are able to claim their entitlements will find that the levels of benefit allocated scarcely enable them to survive, let alone stand any chance of saving money to enter the private rented sector. For example, Shelter has drawn attention to the gap that can occur between the cost of available hostel accommodation and the local maximum ceilings set for such accommodation by regional offices of the Supplementary Benefits Commission. In Sheffield the maximum ceiling for full board in a hostel had been fixed at £12 per week, while the actual cost locally varied between £15 and £16 (*Roof*, 1977); CHAR, (1977) in submitting evidence to the Department of the Environment Review of the Rent Acts pointed out that in central London hostel costs could amount to £1.30 per night for a bed in a cubicle, while the local ceiling for full board in a West End hostel was £23 weekly.

The proportion of a poor person's income needed to meet the cost of available accommodation brings us full circle back to the supply of housing. It is often assumed that single people are likely to experience fewer financial difficulties in housing themselves than are families, on the grounds that a higher disposable income is available to them once the cost of necessities has been met. The Greater London Council and London Boroughs Association (1977b) placed certain important qualifications to this assumption. The report drew on the figures of the Family Expenditure Survey for Greater London for 1972. These showed that a family consisting of two parents and two children had an average weekly income of £58·32 and an average weekly expenditure of £48·39. For that family its average housing costs were 11·5% of its total income and 13·9% of its total expenditure. On the other hand, a single person was averaging an income of £25·91 with a total weekly expenditure of £21·56. For that one-person household, average housing costs represented 19·3% of his income and 23·2% of his total expenditure. The report commented:

> He will be at a disadvantage at the point of entry to owner-occupation or private furnished renting in being able to bring a smaller total of financial resources to bear at the outset; this is when the possession of capital is most important, for example for "fixtures and fittings" in the case of an unfurnished private tenancy . . . costs are also important for those living in lodging houses, hostels and similar kinds of accommodation. The fact that common-lodging houses are in essence cheap accommodation must not be lost sight of, subsidies are needed to avoid increases in charges which would be self-defeating in that they would lead to the creation of some alternative low standard provision.

Government Policy

I have argued that there are two primary causes of homelessness among single poor people: a chronic shortage of accommodation available for single people at a cost which they can afford and at a standard which will afford them the self-respect they seek along with the rest of the population; and drastically reduced employment prospects for poor people who possess few, if any, skills. Since 1965, when the Government conducted a survey into the circumstances of single poor and homeless people (National Assistance Board, 1966) which should have alerted them to these trends, Government policy has been characterised by a failure to arrest these primary causes and a propensity to tinker with their results.

The cardinal criterion of Government policy, as a means of ignoring these primary causes, has been to treat "single homeless people" as a separate, special group of people. Segregation in policy has perpetuated segregated provisions. The outcome of Government policy has been to make it much more difficult for the single homeless poor to obtain equal access to community services and easier for local authorities to resist the requirements of single poor people living in hostel accommodation in their districts.

The 1824–1935 Vagrancy Acts personify the classification of the single homeless poor as a breed of human beings for whom special provisions, in this case special laws, are necessary. Another chapter of this book is devoted to these statutes. However, it must be underlined that the Vagrancy Acts are seen by the Government as a set of laws for a special type of person. Suffice it to quote the image of homeless people which springs from the pages of the Report of the Home Office Working Party on Vagrancy and Street Offences (1974). Debating the need for a criminal sanction against rough sleeping, the report says:

> We have been fully conscious of the views of those criminologists who believe that society should show itself to be more tolerant of deviant behaviour, and should seek ways of "decriminalising" it. There is some force in the argument that sleeping out as such is a harmless activity which may, if the person sleeping out looks unkempt or unprepossessing, raise irrational fears and prejudices . . . we consider that there should not be a criminal law against sleeping out as such.

Then the Working Party gives its reasons for this enlightened decision.

> Such a law would embrace not only overtly unconventional conduct (sleeping out by alcoholics, drug addicts and other misfits) but, for example, sleeping out by holidaymakers who had run out of money, by persons queueing for tickets for entertainments and sporting events, by would-be house purchasers. We do not believe that a law which penalised such conduct indiscriminately would be acceptable to public opinion; and even the tramp habitually sleeping rough may do so harmlessly.

Instead of then advocating the abolition of the vagrancy laws as such, the Working Party proceeded to make the case for a reformed law applicable to "vagrants" only.

General Government policy has pursued identical lines. First, it has assumed that "vagrants" are a class apart who require special, segregated services, and whose problems are so complex that they require intolerable co-ordination between Government departments. Second, it has argued that the complexity of these needs and the difficulties of co-ordination are such as to afford dealing with the needs of "vagrants" a very low priority. Finally, Government policy has been that, in any case, resources do not exist for tackling these needs, particularly at a time of national scarcity, and that, if solutions are to be pursued they can only be sought inexpensively.

Until the passage of the Housing (Homeless Persons) Act 1977 (incidentally the first Act to define homelessness) to which we shall turn later, primary responsibility for the needs of single people who became and remained homeless lay with local social services authorities and, centrally, with the Department of Health and Social Security. This allocation of responsibility permitted provision for the single homeless poor to be considered and made on the assumption not that there were sound economic and structural reasons for poor single people being and remaining homeless, but that their predicament must result from their personal, and in some cases, group pathology. Thus, until 1977 the main governmental initiatives to effect local authority provision for the single homeless poor have been aimed at social and health services authorities. Single homeless poor people have thus been represented to local statutory authorities as people with pathological rather than economic problems.

Even the development of Government awareness that the problems of the single homeless poor would be better addressed by governmental agencies able to supply accommodation and work has been accompanied by the classification of their range of needs as special. For example, since the Housing Corporation and its registered housing associations have become able to extend their housing activities under the Housing Act 1974 and have been allocated more financial resources, their provision of accommodation for single people, let alone single poor and homeless people, has been categorised by the Department of the Environment as "special needs". This term is in fact used to cover all non-family housing provision. The services provided by the state for single poor people who fall foul of the ordinary supply of housing and employment are very distinctly segregated. I shall look briefly at two examples, services provided by the Supplementary Benefits Commission and health services.

The only agency with a statutory obligation towards the destitute homeless person, prior to the Housing (Homeless Persons) Act 1977, was the Supplementary Benefits Commission. The Commission is under no responsibility to provide accommodation, rather as stated in Schedule 5 of the Supplementary Benefits Act 1976, to provide temporary board and lodging in reception centres for "persons of an unsettled way of living" as a means of influencing them "to lead a more settled life". Twenty-one such centres were provided nationally in 1977 with a total capacity of 2570 beds, seven of the centres in London (Hansard, 1977).

That the Commission has recently begun to question seriously whether the statutory obligation placed on it is either realistic or meaningful is an indication that its provision is so segregated as to fail to carry out its avowed objective of assisting homeless individuals into resettlement within the community. In 1976 the Commission's Annual Report stated that:

> many of those who use these centres are citizens of the city or region in which they are living who rarely leave the district, and are no less entitled than their neighbours to the help of their local housing, social and health services. Moreover the loss of cheaper lodgings and hostels in these areas may be largely due to the clearance and development schemes of the local authorities themselves.

More important still, behind the semantic arguments in which the Commission specialises as to whether a "person of an unsettled way of living" is a "single homeless person" lies the reality that homeless individuals are highly resistant to using provision to which they feel a stigma is attached. This is not because the Commission has not tried desperately to improve both the regime and the image of reception centres. Rather, it is because single homeless poor people actually want to be served as individuals with problems rather than problem individuals.

Another way in which reception centres are segregated is that they are not linked with any strategic housing plan within our large cities for meeting the housing needs of single people. Although the report of the Greater London Council and London Boroughs Association (1977) recommended this step for Greater London, so far reception centres provide no guaranteed access from prolonged homelessness for the destitute homeless other than a long stay in one of the centres which allow people to remain in quasi-hospital surroundings.

The Commission is also responsible for the provision of welfare benefits for homeless individuals and single people who live in temporary hostel accommodation. Once again, a remarkable degree of segregation is to be found. At one level the scheme is characterised by its discretion. A homeless claimant who presents himself at a local supplementary benefits office is not entitled by right to receive a cash payment and may instead be directed to a reception centre. This is set out in Section 11 of the Supplementary Benefits Act 1976. At another level, payments to single poor people boarding in a hostel or lodging house can be made by voucher to the hostel management rather than in cash or giro cheque to the claimant, an arrangement to which the vast majority of claimants in the population are not subject. Further, male claimants living in such establishments may find that they have to make their claim at a special "lodging house office" in which they are segregated from other poor claimants in the locality.

In central London the Supplementary Benefits Commission maintains two such special offices for claimants who live in 20 hostels and lodging houses north and south of the Thames. Among the officially stated reasons for maintaining these offices is the following, given in a memorandum to CHAR:

> It is estimated that 85% of the claimants who are dealt with at the lodging house offices are people who are unacceptable to society generally. They include meths drinkers, alcoholics and many of unclean habits. It is accepted that for many reasons they should not be segregated from other claimants, but it is necessary to do so to avoid worsening the conditions for the majority of claimants, particularly for mothers who have to bring young children into our offices.

Although the explicit provision of special offices is confined to London, in other cities it is customary for a particular office to be similarly used by local offices as a point to which to refer homeless claimants.

One further area of statutory provision in which single homeless poor people face severe disadvantages resulting from their virtual segregation is medical care. Prolonged homelessness or dependence on sub-standard lodging house conditions could be expected to result in poor health among homeless individuals. "The health needs of single homeless people are certainly as great as, if not greater than those of the rest of the population", reported CHAR in evidence presented to the Royal Commission on the National Health Service (Davies, 1974; CHAR, 1977b), "certain chronically handicapping illnesses like bronchitis and tuberculosis are much more common". While ailments shared by the majority of the population are to be found to a more significant extent among poor individuals without recourse to a secure environment, a balanced diet and an average standard of living, certain diseases occur to an alarming degree. A survey conducted in Edinburgh in 1975 found the incidence of tuberculosis among residents of the city's lodging houses to be more than five times the average rate for the general population, the death rate from chronic bronchitis was more than double the average rate (McCrory, 1975).

However, against this incidence of ill health, CHAR's report pointed out that "access to medical care is severely restricted. The mobility and stigmatisation of the homeless poor reduce their chances of registering with a general practitioner" (CHAR, 1977b). A Liverpool Community Health Council was cited as reporting that in 1976 six out of ten homeless people in the city were unable to obtain primary medical care from a GP. The Government's own survey in 1972 (Wingfield-Digby, 1976) found that 19% of the male residents of hostels were not registered with a doctor, a further 10% registered with a doctor over an hour's journey away. CHAR's conclusions were:

> The factors influencing the restricted access to a general practitioner by homeless people are first the apparent mobility of the patient in the context of a service geared to static family groups; second the unwillingness of most doctors to accept homeless people as patients; third the isolation of many homeless people and their rejection as outcasts contribute to a low motivation in seeking medical help from the proper source.

This isolation of course prevents equitable access to other health services, none perhaps so vital as the facilities provided for alcoholics by the health service. The main source of referral to the 23 alcohol addiction units in England and Wales is the general practitioner service, and, although they are pitifully inadequate to cope with the demand, they cater almost entirely for the settled community's needs. Among the single homeless population the incidence of alcoholism is high, yet access to these services is severely restricted.

The provision of services for homeless alcoholics brings us to the next characteristic strand of government policy towards the single homeless poor. Having approached their position on the assumption that they are a special group and having provided special, largely segregated services, which have resulted in single poor people finding even greater difficulty in gaining access to ordinary services on ordinary terms, policy makers conclude that the needs of the single homeless are complex and require a high degree of co-ordination between different statutory services. The case of services for the homeless alcoholic serves as an illustration. It is now over ten years since the 1967 Criminal Justice Act was passed to replace in Section 91 the punishment of habitual drunken offenders by the courts with their treatment within the health service. It is seven years since a Home Office Working Party recommended two particular steps to secure this goal, the establishment of two experimental detoxification centres within the health service and the provision of a minimum of 2200 beds in community-based small hostels to cater for the homeless alcoholic (Home Office, 1971). Since then the establishment of the detoxification centres named in the Working Party report has been achieved, although the target number of centres has altered with changes of Government (CHAR, 1976c), but by 1976 only 443 places in the recommended hostels had been set up. Part of the reason for this long delay (we shall deal with another part shortly) has been the effects of the division of responsibilities between the Home Office and the Department of Health and Social Security at national level and the constant need to set up and work through intricate co-ordinating machinery to carry out policy.

An even more horrific example of the results of a strategy of co-ordination occurred recently in the response of government to the needs of young homeless people following the television documentary film "Johnny Go Home" screened in 1975. The Department of Health and Social Security convened a Working Group to make recommendations, which included representatives of six government departments, four local authority bodies and three voluntary organisations. The Working Group reported almost a year after the film had been screened, making recommendations for action by central and local government, aimed at preventing homelessness among young people and meeting the needs of those who become homeless (Department of Health and Social Security, 1976). One year later, after the Government had already indicated that the recommendations of the Working Group could not be implemented if they involved the allocation of new expenditure, the Department of Health and Social Security held a consultative meeting with the local authority associations to discuss implementation. The single concrete decision at this meeting, according to a statement by the Secretary of State for Social Services in the Commons (Hansard, 1977b), was that the associations and his Department would consider the production of a guide for voluntary organisations on the establishment of hostels!

Minority groups are always afforded low priority in the agenda of governments, nationally and locally. The traditionally low priority granted to the single homeless poor is compounded by the strategy of better co-ordination of services, since this must always face separate departments and separate authorities with changes in working patterns and erosions of carefully delineated boundaries of responsibility. Further, if government approaches the position of the single homeless poor without conceding that these men and women might conceivably have rights, it can be anticipated that they will continue to be given very low priority.

The new Housing (Homeless Persons) Act provides a vivid example. Before the Bill was presented to Parliament, Reg Freeson, Minister for Housing and Construction, made clear its objectives in this statement to the Commons on 26th November 1976 (Hansard, 1976a):

> There is no question of every homeless individual having a preferential statutory right among all the other needs reported which have to be dealt with by local authorities. The first claim on resources must go to the most vulnerable, including families with young children.

Despite a moving plea in the House of Lords by Lord Soper that homeless people should not be penalised for having been homeless for long periods (Hansard, 1976b), the Housing (Homeless Persons) Act 1977 reflects entirely the priorities enunciated by Mr Freeson. A hierarchy of claims from homeless applicants is now established in Section 2 of the Act, single people only having a right to accommodation when homeless if they fall within the "deserving" categories of vulnerability through old age, mental or physical disability, or pregnancy. All other single homeless people, no matter how long they have been homeless, are only entitled to receive "advice and appropriate assistance".

This low priority in policy has of course been accompanied by an equivalent priority for financial resources. It is one of the tragedies of the evolution of government policy in the past ten years that as the message has begun to be received by government that the key need of the single homeless poor is for appropriate housing provision, spending programmes on housing have been tightly reined. However, there is such wide agreement throughout the nation that public expenditure must be restrained, that a campaign to improve the intolerable position of single poor people is hardly likely to succeed in any confrontation with this view, and can only hope to put forward the case for different priorities within current spending programmes.

The cornerstone of Government policy to date on directing resources to meet the accommodation and supportive needs of single homeless people has been a heavy reliance on the non-governmental, voluntary sector. Thus, for example, the Home Office, the Department of Health and Social Security and the Supplementary Benefits Commission have for a number of years provided grants to voluntary organisations to maintain night shelters and a range of residential projects specialising in accommodation for offenders, alcoholics, drug users and the long-term homeless. More recently, the extended powers given to the Housing Corporation under the Housing Act 1974 have provided potential for a major expansion of voluntary housing through registered housing associations, while the Housing (Homeless Persons) Act has given the Department of the Environment similar powers to those at the disposal of the DHSS. Local housing and social services authorities can similarly fund local voluntary provision.

The "Directory of Projects", compiled by six voluntary organisations (Camberwell Council on Alcoholism *et al.*, 1976), reflects the results of this policy. Over 1300 projects offering hostel accommodation and other day services for single homeless people in England and Wales are listed, over 800 of which were provided exclusively by voluntary agencies.

Yet as a major cornerstone of the allocation of resources by public authorities, this heavy reliance on the voluntary sector is open to two main criticisms. First, as a strategy to expand services it underestimates the difficulties which small voluntary projects are faced with if they seek to expand their services. One sign of this is that regular Ministerial reply in Parliament that funds have been allocated for services, but that insufficient claim for those funds has been registered by voluntary agencies, hardly an apology for a dynamic policy. Second, the expansion of voluntary services inevitably produces a further stratum of special, labelled and segregated services. The Directory aleady mentioned subdivides the projects listed in two ways: first, according to the length of stay allowed to a homeless person, then and crucially, between services labelled as for the mentally ill, alcoholics, adult offenders or drug takers. Although much of this special provision has an important role to play in meeting the needs of some homeless individuals whose homelessness is now desperately compounded by, say, a chronic drinking problem, as the means of providing housing accommodation for the single homeless poor it can have little useful role. It is, in fact, more likely to confirm the image the public have of single homeless poor people that they are a separate group in society, for whom shifts in the supply of housing and employment would make little difference.

In this section, I have sought to show that Government policies have been aimed at containing the results of the housing and jobs market through a series of age-old statutory services and by offering grants to voluntary agencies to provide a safety net to offset the worst effects of the housing squeeze on the single poor. There have, of course, been important touchstones for the future, of which I name two, one a legislative reality, the other still only a point of policy discussion. The visible switch of central responsibility to the Department of the Environment, and therefore to local housing authorities, for homelessness policy and the passage of the Housing (Homeless Persons) Act are auguries for the future. The growing awareness that the trends in unemployment, particularly as they affect the unskilled, may not be a temporary phase, ought also to provide the basis for a more fundamental attack on the poverty of the unskilled. Overall I believe the time has come for a different approach for meeting the needs of the single homeless poor.

A New Approach

Since the great Reform Act 1832, the progress of underprivileged classes and minorities, indeed the evolution of greater social equality within Britain, has been characterised by a broad process in which rights have been fought from below, and granted from above with sufficient sophistication to prevent a revolution on the one hand or the deliberate starvation of an entire class or group on the other. That is, I know, a generalised simplification of the development of Britain from a less to a more mixed society in terms of wealth and possessions, power and privilege. Yet, for good or ill, it is still a valid simplification to describe the evolution of social goals in the last quarter of the twentieth century, with one proviso. Since the second World War working class earners in general and the labour movement in particular have gained a position in which, for the first time, their incomes and standing can be as much affected by demands from below as by dispensations from above. This change is of particular significance in the struggle to secure improved conditions for the single homeless poor.

The main objective of a campaign for the single homeless poor must be to bring this historic process to bear in their case, in other words to demand rights for single homeless people, and to demand them in such a way as they can be met. The omens for such a campaign are not as bleak as might at first sight appear.

It is true that the single homeless poor have shown a desire to survive against the intolerable daily conditions they face, rather than organise themselves to fight. The fact that, although they are not a homogeneous group, they face constant labelling and categorisation, criminalisation and rejection as undeserving, added to the extreme disadvantages described earlier, does not serve as fertile ground for organised pressure and self-help. Nevertheless, there are the beginnings of a readiness on the part of some homeless individuals to see such organisations as claimants' unions and squatting groups as a positive way of finding allies. Some voluntary organisations, in addition, see their aim in providing accommodation and employment for single homeless poor people as a deliberate attempt to provide a setting in which those who might elsewhere be classed as residents are able to become tenants or co-operative owners, those who might be kept unemployed are provided rate-for-the-job work or invited to participate in a co-operative way in owning the employment scheme. It would be misleading to exaggerate the scope of these trends, but there are the beginnings of consumer awareness, if not assertion.

Further, although the growing voluntary sector is in some ways as anarchistic, independent and entrepreneurial as charitable bodies tend to be, the past few years have seen an influx into the ranks of voluntary organisations of workers whose commitment is not simply to cater for the daily needs of individuals and perhaps thereby increase their dependence on charitable good works, but who are partly concerned with the daily frustrations caused to their project by the lack of suitable housing and work for the single unskilled. One of the interesting trends within the voluntary work force in recent years has been the growth of trades union affiliations among these workers, which of itself could help to widen public debate. Yet a further conscious development within the organised voluntary sector, chiefly through CHAR, has been the building of greater unity with organisations campaigning on behalf of the family homeless and the family poor, so as to reduce the capacity, in the long run, of public authorities to play one priority off against another. The stirrings of self-help and the existence of a growing lobby ready to advocate the cause of the single homeless poor should provide the basis for a new approach.

Three basic rights will form the long-term objective of this approach: the right to decent housing when homeless, the right to a statutory minimum income, and equal civil rights along with the rest of the community.

Segregated, specialised services have been allowed to develop because single homeless people have been denied the right of access to decent housing. The review made earlier in this chapter clearly showed that inequitable access to the national health services and to the welfare benefits scheme derived from, and was reinforced by, the segregation of single homeless people into peculiar forms of accommodation or none. The Housing (Homeless Persons) Act has now established the principle in law that homeless people should have a right to be housed. The task remains to extend its scope to include all single homeless people within that right.

Under the Act all homeless single people can now register their homelessness with a housing authority. Although at this stage such registration is something of a token, at the very least the records of local authorities throughout Britain will, from now on, codify the extent of unmet housing need among the single homeless. That in itself will deter central Government authorities from discounting the degree of need and the necessity for appropriate housing supply.

Once a single person has registered as homeless, Section 9 of the Act provides for housing authorities to bring to bear the resources of all relevant agencies in their areas, not only other local authority departments but registered housing associations, to help meet the needs of homeless applicants. This in itself is likely to concentrate the minds of public authorities and to lead to pressure on their priorities in supplying housing accommodation. Indeed, the hope is that the demands from homeless single people for accommodation under the Housing (Homeless Persons) Act will force local authorities to radically change their supply of housing and their allocations policies so as to take account of the needs of single people. These changes will then pave the way for an extension of the Act itself to provide the right to accommodation to all single homeless people.

No area of public housing policy requires such attention, so far as single people are concerned, as allocations policies. In the last two years certain authorities, led by the Greater London Council, have attempted to cope with demand from single people by circumventing the allocations procedures and letting interwar blocks and other hard-to-let properties to single people on a "ready-access" basis, virtually first come first served. Such schemes can only act as palliatives. What is required in the large cities is a total reassessment of housing needs across the board, followed by the adjustment of present allocations systems which place a priority on family size. It is my own personal view that such changes must take into account the means of a homeless applicant and the duration of that applicant's homelessness.

I would wish to be the last to divert from the ideological approach to homelessness set forward by Lord Soper in the extract from his speech already quoted, or to set the claims of single homeless people over against the claims of, say, homeless families. Of course the long-term objective should be the housing of all our people, irrespective of their "deserts" or their comparative difficulties in the housing market. However, future generations will, I am sure, find fault with our inability to make better use of our scarce resources of housing by not devising systems of allocation which gave priority to all those who had known no secure home for months, if not years, and to those whose means disqualify them from even beginning to compete in the private rented sector or the owner-occupied sector. The development of co-operative housing is so far little advanced and would tend to favour groups of single people with more skills than the hard core single homeless, and it is to public sector allocations that most pressure must be turned.

One indirect result of pressure to implement and extend the Housing (Homeless Persons) Act will be the improvement of conditions in housing to which homeless applicants are referred. As a start, those single people who fall within the Act's priorities will not be able to be placed by councils in substandard housing conditions, and will therefore escape the worst squalors of the lodging-house circuit; in addition, the Act will provide for those individuals outside present priorities who are referred to sub-standard accommodation by a council to bring their conditions to the council's attention and, if no action ensues, to register the necessary complaints with the local public health inspectorate. For all homeless people the Act should provide a foothold for increased public pressure against unacceptable housing standards.

The Protestant ethic has left an indelible conviction in British minds that hard work is the only valid source of income. I have already shown that the trend in employment prospects for the unskilled, let alone the semi-skilled, suggests that a significant change in the economy over the next decade would do little to affect this underlying development. Further, society is at long last debating the need for the economy to be controlled so as to guarantee a greater emphasis on leisure, education and other aspects of life as the necessity for labour-intensive employment diminishes. It is thus highly likely that the debate will soon turn to the question of the public provision of a guaranteed income for those citizens who either cannot work at all within the emerging economy or who can only work part-time.

We have seen that the single homeless poor face serious problems both in securing an adequate income from current welfare benefit levels and indeed in securing such an income at all. We have also seen that, in London, the provision of special methods of claiming for those locked into the lodging-house circuit serves to reinforce their disadvantage. The public acceptance of a basic right to a statutory minimum income, not a statutory minimum wage, would go a very long way to erasing the disadvantaged position of the single poor.

In its submission to the Royal Commission on the Distribution of Incomes and Wealth in 1976, CHAR (1976b) set its target as a statutory minimum income of not less than two-thirds the average male earnings recorded by the New Earnings Survey, which in April 1976 would have produced a minimum of about £50 per week.

Since it is likely that this right will not be conceded for many years, the task in the meanwhile is to remove the separate methods of claiming welfare benefits provided for claimants labelled as single homeless types. In particular, the method of payment by voucher to specified accommodation should be abolished. In 1976 the Supplementary Benefits Commission amended the forms it gives to claimants in receipt of voucher payments to make clear that a claimant is not bound to stay in the accommodation to which a voucher is assigned and can return the form to the lodging house office. The next step should be for payment by voucher to be abolished altogether.

Further, the maintenance of the special lodging house offices in London, together with any such implicit offices in other conurbations, should be brought to an end. Early in 1977 the Commission agreed to a request by CHAR to monitor claims made at the Thames North office for a four week period ending 20 January 1977. Out of a total number of claims met over that period of just short of 5000, the office estimated that 1100 case papers could have been immediately transferred to five different local offices north of the Thames in the case of claimants who had "been in residence for more than a month and who had not caused disturbances". This is a clear indication that an exercise in smooth transfer to ordinary claiming conditions could easily be mounted by the Commission.

The single homeless poor will not achieve equal civil rights alongside the rest of the population until the 1824–1935 Vagrancy Acts are swept into the dustbin of mediaeval history. The recent Home Office Working Party could find no sound justification for the existence or reform of these laws other than that single homeless poor people are a special type of person within the general population. Since all the social and economic factors indicate that this is not the case, and that an attack on the causes of single homelessness alone will diminish the presence of single poor people in our public places, the pretence that the Vagrancy Acts serve in any way to direct the homeless to accommodation and help simply reveals the bankruptcy of official policy.

References

Camberwell Council on Alcoholism, CHAR, Cyrenians, NACRO, NAMH SCODA (1976). "Directory of Projects 1976–7." Barry Rose, Chichester.

CHAR (1976a). "Jobless and Homeless." Memorandum to the Manpower Services Commission.

CHAR (1976b). "Low Incomes of Single Homeless People." Evidence to the Royal Commission on the Distribution of Incomes and Wealth.

CHAR (1976c). "Habitual Drunken Neglect."

CHAR (1977a). Submission to the Department of Environment's Review of the Rent Acts.

CHAR (1977b). "Health Care Needs of Homeless People." Submission to the Royal Commission on the National Health Service.

Commission of the European Communities (1977). "The Perception of Poverty in Europe." Brussels.

Davies, A. (1974). "The Provision of Medical Care for the Homeless and Rootless." CHAR, London.

Department of Environment and Welsh Office (1977). "Housing Policy: A Consultative Document." HMSO, London.

Department of Health and Social Security (1976). "Report of the Working Group on Homeless Young People." DHSS, London.

Erlam, A. and Brown, M. (1976). "Catering for Homeless Workers." CHAR and Low Pay Unit, London.

Greater London Council and London Boroughs Association (1977a). "Provision of Accommodation for Single People: Final Report." GLC, London.

Greater London Council and London Boroughs Association (1977b). "Review of the Housing Needs of Single People in London." Second Report of the Joint Working Party, GLC, London.

Hansard (1976a). Commons, 26 November, Col. 438.

Hansard (1976b). Lords, 30 November, Col. 184.

Hansard (1977a). Commons, 21 July, Col. 698.

Hansard (1977b). Commons, 16 December, Col. 599.

Home Office (1971). "Habitual Drunken Offenders." HMSO, London.

Home Office (1974). "Working Paper of the Working Party on Vagrancy and Street Offences." HMSO, London.

McCrory, L. (1975). "Sick and Homeless in the Grassmarket." Grassmarket Project, Edinburgh.

National Assistance Board (1966). "Homeless Single Persons." HMSO, London.

Roof (1977). Shelter, London.

Supplementary Benefits Commission (1976). "Annual Report 1975." HMSO, London.

Tidmarsh, D. and Wood, S. (1972). "Camberwell Reception Centre: Summary of Research Findings and Recommendations." DHSS, London.

Wingfield-Digby, P. (1976). "Hostels and Lodgings for Single People." Office of Population Censuses and Surveys, London.

The Public Presentation of Vagrancy

PETER BERESFORD

As even the most unimaginative organiser of the humblest skid row agency immediately appreciates, the mass media are an indispensable ingredient in the social policy process, yet little mention is made of them in the literature, almost as though they were judged unworthy of it. The communication of vagrancy, of which they are a crucial element, may offer the key to unravelling the problem, and what begins as an attempt to understand vagrancy, may become a case study raising much larger issues about social problems and social policy generally.

A conventional way of analysing the development of a social problem like vagrancy, is in terms of the conversion of "personal troubles" into "public issues" (e.g. Timms, 1974, pp. 119–130). Whatever complexities this may admit in the passage between the two, it can also commit us to too many preconceptions about the nature and role of social policy. An alternative which takes less for granted and which may follow the actual process involved more closely, is to consider the way in which certain phenomena come to be conceived of as a social problem—why it is, therefore, that certain activities, individuals, institutions and locations, are identified as vagrancy. What we might call the public presentation of vagrancy provides the perspective to do this. It thus becomes possible to see why the phenomena are interpreted as they are, and what the significance and consequences are, both for them and for social policy.

It is important to make this distinction between the phenomena and the social problem in which they are included. While commentators of vagrancy often seem to suggest that all they are doing is describing an independent entity, what they actually seem to be doing is creating one. All that is written and said about the subject becomes the repository of its identity. It acts like a code of instructions, so that if all the apparatus and institutions of vagrancy were to be destroyed; the lodging houses, hostels, hand-outs, shelters, soup-runs, rough sleeping places, day centres, etc., and all we were left with were the people formerly associated with them: the shabby, the homeless, the Irish and Scots itinerant labourers, the city newcomers, etc., the same problem could be resurrected and them fitted into it from this blueprint. Indeed this is what has happened through vagrancy's history, so that now we still conceive of modern issues in terms of this nineteenth century problem. This chapter and book are themselves an inescapable part of that process of social problem construction, although hopefully they will serve to explain rather than compound it.

Recently a view of skid row has been offered as a psychological rather than a physical territory—a state of mind of skid rowers rather than their location (e.g. Archard, 1975). If we are to accept such a psychic interpretation of this province of vagrancy perhaps it should be one that conceives of it not so much in the minds of its inhabitants as the product of the thinking of its formal definers, for skid row is a conceptual construct of its definers first and its inhabitants second. While the latter may give shape to their own world and way of life and put skid-rows' aims and agencies to their own uses, whatever meanings they attach to its institutions and their behaviour, and however important these are, definitions other than their own predominate and are the cause of their being identified as deviant, and skid row defined as a social problem. They are not the authors of the apparatus of skid row, the official sanctions that surround it or the thinking that has inspired them both.

It is not only as a social problem that the phenomena of vagrancy need be ordered. The large lodging houses that are now seen as part of the problem were once envisaged as a solution to it, while reception centres were intended as a remedy rather than one of its receptacles. The realisation that the phenomena might be framed in other ways raises the issue of why they are formulated as they are. It is the large and neglected area of interpretation and formulation between formal problem and the phenomena included in it that requires examination. While certain assumptions clearly underlie skid-row institutions like rehabilitation hostels, day centres and soup-runs, assumptions significantly, which tend to underplay the transactional nature of the problem, there are other less evident ideas and processes at work, ordering and interpreting the disparate phenomena associated with vagrancy and skid row. While recent sociology has alerted us to the idea of social problems being socially constructed, little attention has been paid to the actual process involved in a problem like vagrancy. Interest has largely been restricted to the particular process whereby individuals are identified and dealt with as deviants by agents of control like the police, social workers and rehabilitation agencies.

Lately the tendency has been to emphasise ordinary people's isolation from deviant behaviour in order to explain their dependence on information and definitions of deviance from the mass media (e.g. Wilkins, 1964, pp. 59–65).

It is an argument that seems especially difficult to sustain in the case of vagrancy where most of us are likely to have first hand experience of phenomena included in the problem. A large part of the down-and-out domain is public property—the public places we all frequent—coach and railway terminals, caffs, parks, public lavatories and streets. Living in a city like London, out late in the West End or catching a tube or train home last thing at night, we see men congregating at a soup-run stop or sleeping rough, we are targets to be begged by public drunks and panhandling homeless kids, we move among shabbily dressed men with bags at their feet killing time in public libraries and we can see into the Rowton House and Salvation Army hostel as we are going by on the bus. If we live in the country we know the regular callers at the door, the casual fruit-pickers who come year after year, the itinerant labourers at the side of the road, middle-aged among the young hitchers, and the eccentrics who, living rough and largely self-sufficient, qualify in conventional reckoning for the label of traditional tramp. We ourselves are likely to have done some of the things included in the problem; we may have come to the city with nowhere to go, been temporarily homeless, slept on a friend's or relation's floor or put-u-up, wandered the streets overnight or stayed in a hostel before moving on to a place of our own.

Our dependence on the mass media seems to follow less from a lack of contact with, or knowledge of, vagrancy phenomena, than from a need for negotiators of their meaning and for further information about what we may be encouraged to imagine is a strange world we have chanced upon. If what we seek is the phenomena's true meaning, what we can expect will be conditioned by the nature of the suppliers and their expectations of the demand. What actually seems to happen is that the mass media divorce us from our own experience by imposing their own meaning on the phenomena. The process whereby the phenomena we know become the social problems we are told about, involves pressure groups, mass media and government, with the mass media acting as intermediary between us and the phenomena, and between pressure groups and government. When we speak of the public presentation of vagrancy, we will be referring to a wide and expanding range of media involved in its communication and construction. Running through all of them, organising the phenomena there are two overlapping strands of interpretation that have predominated in the presentation and analysis of vagrancy. Both are closely tied to the *status quo.*

The first and most important strand is best described as that of social control. Vagrancy's interpretation has mainly been by those whose aim has been the eradication of the behaviour included in it and the regulation of those involved. This has been the case from the earliest recorded Anglo-Saxon laws, through the Tudor poor law, the critiques of eighteenth century reformers like Colquhoun and Henry Fielding and the nineteenth century new poor law of the utilitarians, to the present. It is hardly surprising since vagrancy has always served as an umbrella for activities offensive to the state. Thus such a social control interpretation of them commands the resources and authority of the ruling order. If there is any difference in contemporary commentators, it is perhaps that they sometimes seem less aware of the logic or origin of their arguments and that some seem more ambiguous in their aims and loyalties, a point we shall return to later.

Due to the assumption that the behaviour is bad, there is a search for something wrong to explain it. Not surprisingly the search is directed as far away as possible from the social order that initiates it. All sorts of individual ills have been advanced in explanation, according to the culture and causal theories of the age. While moral and mental defect have received the lion's share of credit, a host of others have been suggested according to the purposes and prejudices of their authors. As recently as 1963 Walton-Lewsey (1963, p. 21), telling the story of the London Embankment Mission, an organisation whose hand-outs must be paid for with prayer, explained one Roman Catholic's destitution as due to the "darkness of Romanism". In her study of young crypt users, Holloway (1970, p. 21) seems to have seen some connection in the strange fact that "men who believed in a final Judgement had fewer prison sentences".

The American sociologist, Matza (1969) has traced the effects of such interpretation. Presuming the malevolence of its subject, and concerned only to dispose of it, it denies and pays little attention to its integrity, preoccupied instead with questions of causation. Thus it distorts the phenomena, manipulating them to accord with its own assumptions, ignorant of their actual nature or meaning. Since it is concerned with their solution or control, it presents them as a problem.

A distinction might be drawn between two kinds of social problem conception; that of need and of deviance, mirroring the notions of the deserving and the undeserving. What is included as vagrancy could be framed in either way. The rough sleeper, for example, might be interpreted as either the most acute case of want, or the product of his own inadequacy. While there is some ambiguity in the case of vagrancy, it originates as a problem of deviance, and this is both the parent and the child of a social control interpretation of its phenomena.

The second main strand in the interpretation of vagrancy has come from those Keating (1976) has aptly described as the "social explorers". This tradition where representatives of one class venture forth to report back on the denizens of another below them, has flourished in both the nineteenth and the twentieth centuries, and is a reminder of how much has stayed the same between them. Ostensibly acting as a bridge between rich and poor; middle and working class, it is as much a symbol and reinforcer of the gulf between them. It trades in the lack of communication and contact between the two. The social explorer who puts on tramp's clothing and spends the night in a doss house is news; the thousands whose home it is, are unremarkable. Social explorers report to a "public" that they never seem to imagine extending to the subjects of their exploration. The press campaign preceding the 1972 St. Mungo survey of rough sleepers, emphasised the need for secrecy to prevent people "going to ground", as if it were assumed that they did not read newspapers. Whatever changes it might invite from its audience, social exploration, by its very nature, presumes the maintenance of their existing relationship with the poor and the powerless. It is the power this invests them with that gives it its point, and which it appeals to them to use. Social exploration has always been a genre with literary pretensions. This has not only increased its claim to importance, but also meant that literary demands have had an important effect on its presentation of its subject. "Nearly all" of "Down and Out in Paris and London" is true. These are Orwell's own words (Orwell, 1964). What is presented as fact is blended with fiction (Stansky and Abrahams, 1972, p. 229 *et seq.*).

George Orwell and Jeremy Sandford are the best known of innumerable examples of the school. It is significant that such notable representatives should have turned their attention to vagrancy. It has provided perhaps the most picaresque of subjects for the social explorer's attention.

The accounts of social explorers tend to be presented as the opposite of orthodox social control versions of vagrancy; radical where they are bureaucratic, humane where they are bloodless, lifelike where they are stilted. Chomsky has talked of Orwell "telling it how it was". Sandford is hailed as the advocate of the outcast. Even if we ignore discordant notes like Orwell's fastidiousness, his disdainful talk of "brats", "dirty old habitual vagabonds", "a graceless, motley crew" and his obtrusive upper class ignorance—"but I say, damn it, where are the beds?" (Orwell, 1964, pp. 121, 125, 127, 130), and Sandford's prurience, we may find that outside their rhetoric, theirs are very little different from the official versions of the problem they seem to challenge.

Orwell's experience of being down and out in London was contemporaneous with a government report on the casual wards he visited (Ministry of Health, 1930; Stansky and Abrahams, 1972, p. 229). At first glance the two accounts seem completely contradictory. Orwell's first hand narrative paints a lurid and damning picture compared with the formal and undramatic paragraphs of its rival, but the latter nonetheless tells of cases where conditions were "infamous and intolerable", where "the sleeping accommodation consisted of a shed which could not on a decent farm be considered fit for an animal of any value". For all that, the official committee's conclusions were undoubtedly conservative. But what of Orwell's? Whatever the sweep of his prose, his solution to the problem reflected the narrowness of his analysis:

> Each workhouse could run a small farm, or at least a kitchen garden, and every able-bodied tramp who presented himself could be made to do a sound days

work. The produce of the farm or garden could be used for feeding the tramps, and at the worst it would be better than the filthy diet of bread and margarine and tea. Of course, the casual wards could never be quite self-supporting, but they could go a long way towards it, and the rates would probably benefit in the long run. It must be remembered that under the present system tramps are as dead a loss to the country as they could possibly be, for they do not only do no work, but they live on a diet that is bound to undermine their health; the system, therefore, loses lives as well as money. A scheme which fed them decently, and made them produce at least a part of their own food, would be worth trying.

Much of what he advocated has since come to pass, but it has meant little real change in the problem of vagrancy or the predicament of vagrants.

For Sandford (1971, p. 9) skid row was "the bilges of our society", and being there, tantamount to personal failure: "I wanted to see what life is like at the bottom, for those who have failed". He saw people like his "Edna the Inebriate Woman" as "adult in physical appearance, (but) at the stage of development of children" (Sandford, 1976, p.12). His solution was the creation of more welfare hostels to house them (Sandford, 1971, p. 162). This was exactly the same narrow interpretation of the problem offered by the National Assistance Board report "Homeless Single Persons" (1966, para. 426), a document condemned by voluntary bodies at the time for the conservatism of its approach. Sandford merely offered the established view of single homelessness as a problem of individual abnormality rather than that of inadequate housing its sufferers knew it to be.

As their recommendations reflect, social explorers tend to share the assumptions of a social control perspective. This may explain why they are so often fêted by the establishment they seem to attack. The predictable outcome of their twin loyalties to a social control perspective and their ostensible aim of improving the condition of their subjects, is their tendency to sentimentalise. In their company we encounter "unfortunates" and oddities, rather than people like ourselves. They offer excuses for people's predicament rather than damning the order that engenders it. Although great importance is attributed to social explorers like Orwell, they seem to have little direct effect in changing policy or improving conditions, a connection between the two is more often assumed than sought or found. Instead they seem to serve more as the occasion for an emotional hiccup that gives a specious sense of action and concern. Although it has not shared the same significance in curricula, the government report (Ministry of Health, 1930) did more to improve conditions than "Down and out in Paris and London", whose benefits largely seem to have been restricted to its author. As Sandford (1971) observed, the number of homeless families increased after "Cathy Come Home" (BBC TV programme), children continue to be put into "care" because their parents are homeless and homeless fathers are still segregated from their families.

Social control and social explorer interpretations also share other important deficiencies which lead to distortion of the subject matter. Their exponents are unlikely to be familiar or have close contact with it, coming from a different class and culture to the subjects of most social problems. They are predominantly middle-class interpreters of working-class phenomena. They are unlikely to be familiar with their subjects' own interpretation of their circumstances. The social explorer makes brief excursions into the milieu; the social controller may never visit it at all, or if he does, only see as much as his role allows. This class difference and the isolation between the classes are the *raison d'être* of social exploration. It is perhaps more than a coincidence that both Orwell and Sandford were Etonians. Everything conspires against an adequate understanding of the subject or its thorough observation. Neither perspective is committed to giving a full account of it. One is concerned to obliterate it; the other to shape it to its own literary purposes. Social control analysis isolates itself even further from its subjects by the way it studies them, looking at them in isolation and using research techniques like structured interviews and tests that alienate them even further. There are also strong pressures on both to emphasise the strangeness of their subject. The social controller looks for individual abnormalities to explain the problem he imputes. The social explorer is tied to a form that relies for its appeal on accounts of the extraordinary and outlandish. It is in the nature of social exploration to dramatise and sensationalise. The mundane can have no place in its attraction.

Where once it was the criminal and poor law that shaped the problem of vagrancy, it is now the statutory and voluntary welfare agencies, inheriting their role of social control, which are its main purveyors. Most commentators are still recruited from them. This is hardly surprising since it is essentially only the apparatus of social control they constitute that offers the opportunities and employment. They are the source of the social control perspective that defines the problem. It is embodied in a specialist literature of research studies, campaign reports, annual reports and house magazines of the agencies involved, books, official statistics and parliamentary papers, as well as contributions in the social service press and journals. Voluntary body annual reports have their own peculiar style; a curious blend of self-written reference and begging letter. An almost Victorian self-righteousness still sometimes permeates their pages (St. Mungo Community Trust, 1971):

> To see a man change from a shambling near-wreck suffering from malnutrition and hopelessness who was shunned by all except us, to being a happy person with a new sense of dignity who cannot do enough to help others is PROOF that the methods we use do work . . . You will see how economically we can keep and help people at £2 per week.

Social administration text books, which seem to have little other use but to serve as a source of received and institutionalised knowledge for those

joining the ranks of the social problem process, are coy of mentioning
vagrancy, but reveal their tacit acceptance of the conventional view of it by
the way they discuss homelessness as a family problem (Mays *et al.*, 1975,
Brown, 1976).* Research has been fettered to the conventional concerns of a
social control perspective (see DHSS, 1975). Of ten books about vagrancy in
Britain published since 1966, only one could be said to be truly outside the
social control tradition of interpretation (Archard, 1975). The authors have
been researchers and journalists, but mainly welfare workers. Publishers
clearly believe that there is a market for accounts by welfare workers that
are as much autobiography of the "I have ventured forth into the cess-pits
of our society" variety as accounts of the problem itself (Wallich-Clifford,
1974, 1976; Brandon, 1974). It is another expression of the conjunction
between social control and social explorer streams of interpretation.

Such specialist sources are only the first stage in the formulation of
vagrancy, although in many ways they have a deciding influence on the final
shape it takes. After them come the mass media. Clearly there is an overlap
between them, but there is a real difference in kind; for example, between the
small circulation research report and the popular press feature. The relation
of the two is crucial and complex. The nature of the mass media conditions
the way it works and also influences the specialist sources themselves. Much
of the specialist material is only produced or given its particular form in
anticipation of the mass media response to it. If it is the specialist sources that
generate formal accounts of the problem, it is the mass media that make the
public problem. They are of commanding importance. It seems all the more
strange, therefore, that social problems do not seem to have been considered
much in terms of the process of their communication, since they are not only
social in nature but also in construction. The social problem concept cannot
be disassociated from the means of its transmission.

To understand the effect of the mass media on the interpretation of the
phenomena and their role in the presentation of the problem, it is necessary
to understand how they work. We must take account of them as a social
institution and mass communication as a social process. While all their other
expressions are involved in vagrancy's presentation, news reporting is the
central dimension where the paths of mass media and social problem cross.

One of the few things said about the mass media and vagrancy is that their
news treatment of the problem is hostile. In fact for every condemnatory
story, there seems to be another lauding efforts to aid or rehabilitate vagrants.
It is not this kind of crude bias that is central to the mass media's presentation
of vagrancy. The mass media still seem to hold to a view of themselves as the

---

* Mays *et al.* (1975) has no mention of vagrancy in its index, but under homeless, says
"*see* Families (homeless)". Similarly the 3rd edition of Brown (1976) has no mention of
vagrancy, but only talks of homelessness as a family problem.

neutral communicators of objective truth. It is in these terms that they answer complaints against their news reportage. (For example, see the statement from the deputy editor of the BBC TV News, *Radio Times*, 3–9 Sept. 1977, p. 67, rejecting objections against BBC TV News reportage of the counter-National Front demonstrators, 13 Aug. 1977. See also subsequent correspondence *Radio Times* 24–30 Sept., p. 69 and 1–7 Oct., p. 79.) But the bias, if we can call it that, is of a different order. Reality is not a commodity that can be transferred to the news page or programme, of necessity what we call the news is artificially shaped. What it does is restructure and reinterpret reality. This goes for vagrancy as for everything else. There has been a reluctance among those involved in the process to look at it carefully and admit or examine their assumptions. This process is important for the presentation of vagrancy as it involves a variety of constraints which affect the version of reality offered. These conspire to confirm the dominant specialist interpretation of the phenomena, they also extend to other forms of mass media. They are not the kind of restraints that a conspiracy theory of the mass media might presuppose—censorship of stories or directives from above—they have more to do with the way in which the media work and what we might call the ideological air we breathe: "that atmosphere which comes off the morning radio news and chat programmes" (Hoggart, 1976, p. x). News has to be selective and this cannot be a neutral process. Instead it is determined culturally and by the news process itself, within the framework of what has been called "the professional routines and values of 'news-making' " (Hall, 1974, p. 20). The news-maker, consciously or otherwise, absorbs the unstated rules of what is news and then seems to forget that there were ever any to learn, "you just know what makes a story". The formal news values that shape selection constitute an ideological structure for the mass media definition of reality (Hall, 1973, p. 77). They offer us an organising idea for understanding the mass media's treatment of vagrancy phenomena.

They are most clearly expressed in the stock stories of vagrancy, which include tributes to existing welfare agencies and pleas for more: the "community that gives dossers a second chance" (*South Western Star* 27 Oct. 1972); reports of residents' protests against perceived problems or planned projects; and patronising silly season or sentimental tales that keep things in comfortable perspective like: "Tribute to the lonely tramp" (*Daily Mail* 7 Jan. 1977)*:

> Cyril Griffin, the tramp who died a lonely death at Christmas had more friends than he knew . . . Among the wreaths and bunches of flowers was one signed by eight children to whom he had become a familiar sight in shop doorways in Sheffield.

---

* Another media favourite is the tramp who stumbles upon, or on his death, is found to have had a fortune. A man I met staying at the Brighton Reception Centre had kept just such a story of a Scotsman and showed it to everyone, like a talisman.

F

While we cannot offer an adequate account here for the predominance of particular news values, we can see their effects on the mass media's interpretation of vagrancy.

News is concerned with exceptions and the unusual. It either seeks extraordinary subjects or emphasises the extraordinary in others. Thus we can expect it to be interested in vagrancy simply because it sees it as extraordinary, and for its approach to it to be conditioned by this expectation. This may help to explain why vagrancy has always attracted mass media interest disproportionate to its apparent size or importance. Thus vagrancy which conspicuously contains a heterogeneous collection of phenomena which are not readily typified, is characterised by those that are most strange and least representative. This serves to reinforce the conventional interpretation of vagrancy in terms of individual abnormality by encouraging its emphasis. Similarly it encourages the social explorer approach to interpretation, which we should remember has always been, at least in part, a journalistic tradition. (See for example, *The Times* 27 Oct. 1972: "there was no space to sleep under the bridge so I moved on again; Pat Healy our Social Services Correspondent, shares for a night the lonely, tiring life of the 10,000 rootless drifters and down-and-outs who exist in London".)

Interrelated with its emphasis on the unusual, is the news's tendency to dramatise. Both, like other news values, seem to be linked to news's uncertain stance between informing and entertaining. As the organiser of a fund-raising agency in the vagrancy field saw it, "the media as a whole are only interested in 'drama'". When it published a report (pers. comm., 28 Jan. 1977) charting changes in the problem and asserting among other things an increase in the number of homeless girls:

> the one thing that everyone in the media, regardless of whether they were from the popular press, BBC or the more intellectual papers, was most interested in was to find a homeless young woman who was pregnant and to interview her, photograph her etc.

Such an approach leads the news-makers to simplify their subject. They shape it to fit their own needs. They are unlikely to be receptive to complexities or uncertainties which would qualify their account, especially those which blur or conflict with their common-sense view of the phenomena. Thus (pers. comm., 28 Jan. 1977):

> Most reporters, be they press, television or radio, always require a precise figure and are mostly unsympathetic to such things as "it is estimated . . ." and "there could be as many as . . ." and such indications of the uncertainty of the size of the problem.

> One of the most difficult things we find is explaining to the media that the term of "no fixed address" although classed as single homeless does not necessarily

mean that these people are sleeping rough; to the media single homeless and N.F.A. automatically means sleeping rough 365 days of the year.

Best known of all news values is "human interest" and human interest in the news means personification. By personifying issues it can make them clear and concrete and fit them into both its own and its audiences' existing common-sense assumptions about the world. Thus we have:

New bid to block "dossers" centre (*South London Press* 6 Aug. 1976)
"Cardboard box kids" need help says M.P. (*Evening Standard* 1 Aug. 1975)
My Life as a Runaway by Judith, 15 . . . Added Judith, who wants to be an actress: If any other girls are thinking of running away from home, after my experience I should say that they should think very seriously about it (*Daily Express* 24 Feb. 1975).

Personification leads to personalisation. People are made the focal point of the phenomena, diverting attention from their other aspects, which are then only seen through them. Vagrancy is presented as a problem of people, not of conditions or social institutions. In a sense the concept of vagrancy already represents a personalising of the issues included in it. This news value compounds this. It works in conjunction with other news values to confirm conventional individualistic interpretations of the phenomena. It means that vagrancy comes to be presented through a narrow set of stereotypes that follow closely those of specialist accounts of the problem; of inadequates needing care and attention or sociopaths requiring restraint.

News, not least because of its own frequency, is preoccupied with topicality; with the day to day, the immediate. It is concerned with *events* and particularly with what has been called the "event as news": reporting events and those aspects of events that fit its existing definition of the situation (Halloran *et. al.*, 1970, p. 90). It is this that prompts the agency organiser's observation that (pers. comm., 28 Jan. 1977):

Experience has shown me (and three months working in a television newsroom has confirmed this) that whatever is said, the media will only say what they want to say, regardless of what the press releases or the person being interviewed has really said.

This preoccupation with events tends to exclude consideration of background developments and the issues involved. Such things might have a place in news features, but vagrancy is unlikely to have high priority here. It is already competing for space for news. For background features it must compete with a wide range of social concern and social services subjects that are likely to have a prior claim on the attention of the news-maker.

This emphasis on events bodes badly for vagrancy. It means that for it to become news, it must be presented as a series of events rather than the set of phenomena of which it actually consists. This accords ill with the nature of the phenomena. As stated by Hall (1973, p.182) "news stories are concerned with *action*", but vagrancy demarcates an area that is essentially uneventful, where little happens or is likely to be experienced as happening. It encloses a world of queueing, waiting, killing time; a routinised world where people are passed through procedures that make scant allowance for their individuality. Incidents that may seem remarkable to the outsider; sleeping rough, destitution, arrest, court appearance, imprisonment, are more likely to be defined as unremarkable by those involved.

It is the fact that vagrancy is only likely to make news if it is framed as a series of events that leads us to the complex symbiotic relationship there is between the mass media and the voluntary bodies involved in vagrancy. It is a relationship common across the spectrum of social problems, but especially evident in the case of vagrancy. Vagrancy is a problem traditionally dominated by voluntary action, where subsidiarity notions of social policy still predominate. It is essentially a nineteenth century problem with a social policy response still framed in nineteenth century terms. It is these agencies which have been central in the formulation of vagrancy and in the feeding of information to the mass media. The naïve notion of news has the media going out and getting it. Instead they rely on existing accounts. They are dependent on intermediaries. In vagrancy, they place a heavy reliance on voluntary bodies for information, absorbing their version of the problem in the process. The reliance of these agencies on the mass media, on the other hand, has followed as much from their own needs as those of the group they are supposed to serve.

We will begin to understand their involvement with the media once we appreciate their preoccupation with their own position and solvency. Their own poverty and insecurity breed a preoccupation with money and status, especially when they coincide with the strange, sometimes disturbing figures this field seems to attract. Such agencies exist in a competitive and often uncooperative world of scarce resources. They are often as much concerned to press their own claims for attention and investment from government and charitable trust as those of the cause they ostensibly represent. The two interests are often confused. The media are crucial to the agencies for the part their publicity can play in legitimising them and their version of the problem, gaining them resources and ensuring their survival. Thus there is a readiness to structure their version of the problem to fit the demands of news to ensure its coverage. This process whereby they tailor their message to accord with their expectations of the media's requirements can only exacerbate the distortion of the phenomena.

It sets in train an ascending spiral of misrepresentation that reinforces the mass media's own preconceptions of the problem. Agencies personalise the problem, serving up readily recognisable cultural stereotypes. They present it as a series of events, manufacturing events to do so. Thus they feed in "Christmas treat" stories: "Christmas Day dinner for 1500 down-and-outs"

(*South Western Star* 24 Dec. 1971), "A warm room for them at the inn" (*The Guardian* 27 Dec. 1972) (see Beresford, 1974; Stewart and Stewart, 1978) because Christmas is the media season for schmaltz. The readiest means they have of structuring the problem in this way, is by producing reports. Such reports, intended more as media fodder than documents in their own right, which in the past have often been flimsy and inaccurate, containing garbled accounts and little if any new information, are most likely to be framed in terms of crisis. They tell of a problem in a permanent state of crisis, for crisis is news. In news terms they serve as pot-boilers, keeping the issue or agency alive, but they lead to a crisis solution approach to social policy for vagrancy which provokes a semblance of action, but discourages radical reassessment or change.

Agencies have colluded in the same way over the scale of vagrancy. It is always presented as a large and growing problem. It is not only that the larger the problem the more resources they can claim, but that size is a central news value. Thus the one occasion to my knowledge (prior to the appalling winter of 1978–1979) when vagrancy, rather than the scandals surrounding it, became an item of national BBC TV news, was the 1972 voluntary body survey of rough sleepers, when grossly inflated figures were offered. Such an event structured to include a number of subevents: recruiting volunteers, the actual survey, the results, provided a running story—the ideal of both agency and media.

The way the media get their news also conditions the kind of account of vagrancy they offer. Thus a newspaper like *The Guardian*, for example, largely obtains its account of the problem from the press releases, press conferences and personal contacts of the agencies involved (pers. comm. Hugh Hebert, Social Services Correspondent, *The Guardian* 2 June 1977). A local paper like the *South London Press*, on the other hand, places little reliance on press releases. Instead it gets most of its stories from the contacts and complaints of its readers, who see it as a source of aid and advice, with the power to get things done that they themselves conspicuously lack (pers. comm. Christine Rouse, *South London Press*, 30 May 1977). The same seems to be true of a popular national like the *Daily Mirror*. Most of its stories on homelessness come from such contacts, often originating from its readers service department or from court cases (pers. comm. between Leo White *Daily Mirror* and John Bloxsom, 1977). This helps explain why a paper like the *South London Press* is sometimes seen as having a hostile approach to vagrancy and its agencies, because it begins with reports and thus reinforces ordinary people's concerns, confusions and prejudices about the problem as it affects them. Thus these headlines appeared in 1976: "Stop Bermondsey going bad", "Residents, council hit Salvation hostel plan", "DoE approves Salvation hostel plan", "New bid to stop plan for Salvation hostel", "Hostel rebuilding: send homeless to country, suggests councillor". If the meanings it tacitly attaches to the phenomena are those of local residents—and for this reason it is likely to be more democratic than more liberal accounts—the quality press, on the other hand, pass on the conventional, ostensibly progressive, specialist account. The two are however, essentially both sides of the same coin of overlapping specialist and common-sense accounts of vagrancy, personified by the stereotypes of dangerous drop-out and helpless inadequate. Significantly, whatever their conventional political allegiance, the media largely present the same conventional view of vagrancy.

Equally important is the part that visual imagery plays in the presentation of vagrancy. As Barthes (1972) has observed, "pictures . . . are more imperative than writing, they impose meaning at one stroke, without analysing or diluting it". Photographs offer images without insight; they have been especially important in vagrancy. William Read, "a Vagrant examined before a committee of the House of Commons, in the year 1846" still stands looking dolefully out at us from Ribton-Turner's nineteenth century history of vagrancy, tastefully arranged, broom in hand, against a studio backdrop of trees and plaster plinth (Ribton-Turner, 1887, p. 257). Photographs have changed little since, except in sophistication. Vagrants are still offered as exhibits. Vagrancy has been summed up by a narrow range of "stock shots"; the visual clichés media people draw upon to convert the phenomena into a set of readily recognisable images. If the prevailing image in the 1960s was the lurching East End meths drinker, so far in the seventies it has been the cardboard boxes and polythene sheets enclosing West End rough sleepers. Rough sleeping has long been made the predominant image of vagrancy, however unrepresentative it is of what is actually included in the problem.

Photos serve to confirm and give credibility to the conventional or common-sense interpretation of the problem. They are subject to the same news values as the news itself. They play a crucial role in personalising issues. The image becomes more important as a symbol than for its subject. Usually in this field, the photographer has encountered his subject without familiarity or understanding. His approach has been an extension of a social control perspective, treating him as object; Don McCullin's familiar series of sixties' shots epitomises this. How much is the resignation and hostility in the eyes of his crude spirit drinkers a statement about them and how much about him? The vagrant is treated as public property. His face and misfortune are no longer his own. In this, as in other things, his privacy is denied. Men and women who have long left skid row and the degradation they may associate with it, can find stock shots of themselves still in circulation, looking up at them from papers, books and journals, for all their family to see.

It is perhaps the documentary which is the most developed form of mass media account of reality. It at once provides an accumulating context for subsequent interpretations and offers the most detailed expression of the dominant view of the problem. One of the things that distinguishes documentary from straight news reportage and features, is its admission of "imaginative response". John Grierson, coiner of the term and pioneer of the medium, defined documentary as the "creative interpretation of actuality". For all its founder's honest admission of subjectivity, this places a burden on documentary makers which they have conspicuously failed to carry in the case of vagrancy. A documentary becomes a document—more or less significant according to the authority invested in it—but it does not document reality. The documentary makers have fudged this important distinction. As Cameron (1977) has said, it begins as a record, implies an intention and becomes an interpretation. Either by implication or clear statement they have been reluctant to offer their product as less than the truth and failed to make clear their own part in the proceedings. Documentary now mainly means television documentary, thus we are talking as much about the grammar and professional ideology of television as of documentary itself.

Vagrancy has been a popular subject with the documentary makers. British film catalogues list eight recent examples with titles like "The Foxes have Holes", "Soup Run" and "Christmas Down and Out".* Originally made for television, they are now recycled to serve as teaching and training aids, becoming an important part of received wisdom about the phenomenon. In vagrancy's case the apparent paradox between Grierson's view of documentary as a means of informing and educating the people for their role in a mass democratic society—a role which still seems to be seen for it—and its subsequent reputation as socially critical (Lovell and Hillier, 1972, p. 20), may be resolved when we look at the reality of documentaries on the subject. They are essentially conservative in nature. While their posture is invariably liberal and benign, they mainly owe their account to the correctional agencies and they are largely focused on the latter's activity. Nothing here to challenge our common-sense assumptions. In these films we can see the rehabilitation work of the Salvation Army among the "dossers", a Christmas party for "dossers" organised by St. Mungo's where "no one tries, against their will, to clean them up or make them do anything", learn of the "dedicated people trying to help, running hostels", and hear "dossers" retell stories they've told to countless social workers, probation officers and givers of alms.

Documentary might be defined ideally as a compression or the essence of reality, but its makers often have little idea what the "reality" is, usually only coming to it second-hand through the mediation of the agencies involved. It is these agencies they largely rely on to put them in touch with the

---

* British National Film Catalogue, Vol. 13, 1975: "Soup Run", "The Low Road". British National Film Catalogue, Vol. 14. No. 4, December 1976: "Benny". Concorde Films 1974 16mm Catalogue, and Combined supplement to the 1974 edition, March 1976: "Christmas Down and Out", "The Foxes have Holes", "No Fixed Abode", "No Room at the Doss House", "Lucky".

phenomena, thus missing the less visible and less accessible. They only seem to see vagrants as their subjects rather than the whole world in which they are involved. Thus agencies are accepted as part of the solution rather than as another part of the problem.

"Johnny Go Home", the archetypical vagrancy documentary, first shown in 1975, shows the medium in microcosm (Deakin and Willis, 1975). Ostensibly concerned with the issue of young people's homelessness, it presents it in terms of two simple stereotypes; Annie who:

> ran away from home when she was twelve and has lived rough ever since, so she has survived on the street for four years. Annie has been a drug addict, but now at 16 she lives by "tapping"—begging in Piccadilly.

and Tommy:

> ran away from home in Glasgow for the third time but new to London . . . Tommy heads for Piccadilly. Like most runaway kids he's drawn by the bright lights and excitement.

Thus it upholds the news values of personalising its subject and emphasising the extraordinary. It perpetuates the conventional portrayal of the problem as one of individual abnormality when the mass of evidence is against it. The implicit assumption that young people's homelessness is a matter of migrating drop-outs, is confirmed by the documentary's later focus on homosexual prostitution, delinquency and drug use. The unspoken justification for this emphasis on deviant worlds is that this is the fate that awaits kids who leave home.

The documentary offers spurious statistics, dignified by the authority the medium lends: "unbelievably there are probably 25,000 homeless youngsters in London". Voyeurism parades as social enquiry when the interviewer asks the boy who joined the "meatrack": "just tell me exactly what happened that evening . . . tell us about how you felt, uh, the first time in Playland". Despite its play on authority's heavy-handedness, "Johnny Go Home's" own social control perspective occasionally betrays itself in the slogan sentences it owes to the yellow press:

> Tommy's new found friends rapidly introduce him to the twilight world of Piccadilly . . . In the heat of an improvised bonfire in the old Covent Garden, the kids, the drifters and the down-and-outs gather in a way that's hardly changed since Dickens's time. For these people it is a place of instant friendship.

We see cardboard boxes stir as Tommy wakes up on the street in the morning. Did the camera crew really wait all night just for that moment and not set it up? Was it by accident that they were in the Euston Station monitoring room when Tommy came into view on the screen? We see Annie begging on the street and then she tells us that she's living in a commune. Was it all restaged for the camera?

The documentary's subjects are reduced to amateur actors who tell us more about the way they were directed than about themselves. "Johnny Go Home" is part of a school that still insists that: "to present something as it happens it is necessary when filming to rig and recreate" (Bakewell and Garnham, 1970, p. 179). Tommy does not notice the camera, although we may sense him play to it. Nor do other participants. The denial of its presence reflects a greater denial of the documentary's own viewpoint and interpretation. When Tommy returns home to his family who are supposedly seeing him for the first time, having had no idea where he's been, they open the door, greet him, show no surprise at the camera, give no sign of seeing its crew, but leave the door open after him to let them through. It is as if there were a convention that none of us is supposed to know the camera is there. The audience is expected either to be naïve or to suspend its disbelief. It must at once understand this hackneyed and deceitful grammar of documentary and yet not acknowledge it. This contrasts with a new view of documentary, encouraged by the use and techniques of video, where the camera openly interacts with its subject and is often in the hands of those it shows.

"Johnny Go Home" began as just another conventional account of vagrancy, promising the usual puff for the agency involved. It was only by accident, as it tells us, that it hit on another angle to the story: "what neither Tommy nor we knew at that moment was that Gleaves (the agency's organiser) had a long criminal record including indecent assaults on young boys". Now it was no longer primarily concerned with "homeless children", but with "THE social scandal of our time" (blurb in Deakin and Willis, 1976). This provided the kind of event that could be used to justify the major media affair it became.

Thus it reduced young people's desire for independence—the working class equivalent of the middle class leaving home for university—with all its associated structural issues of unemployment and the labour market, social and regional inequality, the nature of the family and the extended childhood role in our society, to a matter of runaway kids and the dangers awaiting them in the big city. It makes it possible for such issues to be defused completely.* Correspondingly, policy could be whittled down to a matter of providing information booths at railway termini and printing posters and leaflets telling adolescents "Why not go to London".

What effects did "Johnny Go Home" have? One immediate answer is offered by the need to make the subsequent "Goodbye Longfellow Road" two years later, recounting another tale of corruption and abuse in the field

---

* See *Sunday People* 9 Oct. 1977, front page headline. "Johnny Go Home" Shock: "Tommy Wylie, star of the sensational TV documentary 'Johnny Go Home' is back with the bogus bishop whose vile sex record was exposed in the film . . . He's happy to be living again with the bogus bishop in a bed-sitter.

of vagrancy.* It did not stop the scandal it chanced upon, although it blamed others for not doing so. Why had it not known about the activities of Gleaves? They were common knowledge in the field. Indeed, it could be said that it was documentaries like "Johnny Go Home" was originally conceived to be, that made regimes like Gleaves' possible, for they could be used by agencies as a stick with which to beat any local or central government authority which was slow to grant them resources or accept their *bona fides*. "Johnny Go Home" was essentially retrospective, defining the present in terms of the past. Much of what it showed was already in the past. The Gleaves affair had been dealt with by the law. Tommy's and Annie's lives had taken different turns. What it did was legitimise all this as a public issue. The murder trial passed off with relatively little media attention. It was the documentary about it that made the headlines.

The contradictions and deceptions of documentary are taken to their logical conclusion by its derivative drama documentary, of which vagrancy has a pre-eminent example in "Edna the Inebriate Woman" (Sandford, 1976). In print the play may only have a minority market of two or three thousand people (3000 copies were printed, pers. comm. Marion Boyars 22 Feb. 1977) but on television it becomes a backcloth for all our thinking, even if it seems to have little profound effect on public attitudes (Beresford, 1977). Nine and a quarter million people saw it on its first showing alone (pers. comm., BBC Audience Research Unit, 13 July 1977—first shown on 21 Oct. 1971). How many will read this book? Theatrical criteria rather than its own nature now play the deciding role in the way a subject is presented. Thus the producer explaining why a comedienne was chosen for the title role wrote (in Shubik, 1975, pp. 89, 132):

> If Edna were too down-beat and tragic, the production might become un-bearably depressing. . . . Equally if Edna had just been ugly, smelly, and a nuisance, without being funny, it would have been difficult to arouse people's sympathy for her plight . . . There is a certain level past which many people do not wish to be disturbed.

Hailed as a bridge between information and entertainment, drama docu-mentary usually comes out badly by the criteria of both. The artistic limitations of writers like Sandford mean that they must dramatise their subject to convey its drama. For all its up-market audience, "Edna" contains the conventional quota of sex and violence that the publicist's eye rather than its subject demands. What it seems to offer is a version of reality that conforms to middle class commentators' expectations and hopes. Thus the producer wrote (Shubik, 1975, p. 125): "It contained a marvellously vivid picture of Dickensian low-life in modern times". Significantly, where

---

* "Goodbye Longfellow Road—A crisis in the Cities", John Willis, Director, Yorkshire Television, 8 March 1977.

"Cathy", the symbol for family homelessness, was faulted for being too respectable and too glamorous, the symbol for homeless single people was an alcoholic vagrant. It is a reminder of how differently the two formal problems are conventionally conceived and the part the mass media have played in reinforcing this distinction and polarisation of problems.

Shubik (1975, p. 102) offered unintended confirmation of the inevitably correctional view of plays like "Edna" when she said that: "no amount of humanizing the social workers disguised the fact that they were mouthpieces for the author". The solution we are offered is one that means nothing needs to be changed. We only need planning permission from that safe, abstract enemy—bureaucrats (Sandford, 1976, p. 100):

> Josie (the social worker) "The answer, so I believe most sincerely, is in the sort of hostel that we have set up. Let us help them. They can exist and be happy in a hostel like ours. They *can* live fulfilled lives. There should be hostels like this everywhere. One every four of five streets."

All these elements we have discussed are not only concerned with the presentation of vagrancy, they are also inextricably involved in the formation and development of policy. Until recently social policy writers have shied away from discussing the details of this process, but there seems to be a common-sense view, which many of us may share, of how it works. Some problem is discovered, perhaps a report is written, it is reported by the media, there is public concern, and the government has to act. If we think about it, it is a model of how our democracy works. Its assumptions seem to run through much of the literature and campaigning of vagrancy. "Johnny Go Home", for example, was said to have "caused an uproar with the public" (Deakin and Willis, 1976, p. 9). This is part of a more generalised notion of documentary as a "catalyst operating the mechanisms of social awareness and change". But on closer examination, what does this actually mean? How do we measure such public alarm and connect it with policy change? The answer is we do not. Instead such unconsidered assertions act as an alternative to proper consideration of the process involved. However, it is a process which requires closer examination and one which raises fundamental questions about the nature of social problems and social policy.

The process the outsider sees of pressure group reports demanding government action, emerges as a stage battle that offers only an exterior view of what actually takes place. Although they affect it, the events these reports represent do not reflect the true process of policy formation. Instead they are merely peaks in a continuing process of negotiation. Government and pressure group are likely to be in regular contact and their representatives on familiar terms. Their actual positions are unlikely to be as opposed as they appear to the outsider and as the mass media make them seem. The shock report is more likely to be symbolic than anything else. Government representatives are likely to be familiar with what it has to say from the pressure group involved. The latter know that out-of-the-blue publicity can be readily dealt with by a bogus show of activity and that publicity without a close relationship with government can mean that policy change is erratic and uncertain. What the report does is give formal notice that its subject is now legitimised as a public issue. Now central or local government department knows that it cannot ignore the issue and must respond to it, however marginally. Government agencies which left to themselves might take the line of least resistance, are constrained by the outside pressure they feel the media impose. The government officer who seeks the same policy as the pressure group now has a means of applying pressure on his department.

But where are the people in all this? At first glance the whole process seems like a strange, ritualised dance of expectations with nothing to compel the moves that actually take place. The "public" is involved only as an abstract and unreal entity. There is no way of summoning it, of hearing its views, or of being restrained by it; but if this public is inaccessible, powerless and fugitive, there is another of much more compelling character. This is the public in Parliament, those who fill the letter page of *The Times*, the senior civil servants and local government officers, councillors and others of the decision-making elite. It is this public that counts in the process of social policy formation, and which the quality press always seems to have at least half, and pressure groups almost entirely, in mind.

Thus the account of a social problem like vagrancy that pressure groups feed to the mass media, can be read at two levels because it is addressed to two audiences; those involved in the decision-making process, and the stage army of the rest. If the latter take it at face value, they are likely to be deceived. For those involved in the social policy process, though, it signifies something different, and it is this meaning that matters for policy. The way in which pressure groups present the problem is conditioned by a strategy of pressing for change from government by holding the spectre of public reaction over it. By doing this, rather than actually involving the people in the social policy process, they alienate them even further from understanding or involvement.

Three important issues arise from this. The process of social policy formation gives a false impression of public participation. It is basically undemocratic. The government/mass media/pressure group process serves as an alternative to democracy. The public plays no direct part in it. Pressure groups are the nearest we have to representatives. When it comes to the detailed formulation of policy, our elected representatives are more closely connected to the other parties in the process than to their electors, and their influence is limited by the importance and the power of the bureaucracies. But pressure groups are neither democratic nor truly representative, either of the general population or of their particular interest group. No vagrancy pressure group has ever had a mandate from skid row.

Those involved in the social policy process of vagrancy are unlikely to be close to their subject. Secondary sources, official inspections and guided tours rather than first hand familiarity have tended to be the rule for government and the mass media. The demands on those in voluntary body pressure groups make it difficult for them to keep close to the field if they are to be effective in the social policy arena—as does the physical and psychological gulf between the two. As we have seen, media people are unlikely to be in close touch with the phenomena and even in their dealings with the agencies involved, they are more likely to have contact with their directors and spokesmen than field workers. Furthermore, none of the three; government, mass media or pressure group, is likely to include anyone from skid row.

Skid rowers' own account of vagrancy and its phenomena rarely gets presented. The primacy of the social control perspective and restrictions on access to the mass media, collude in this. The views of those involved are only likely to be imported when they confirm the conventional account of the problem. When such people are given a chance to express their view, it is usually only as poacher turned gamekeeper (literally in the case of Hill, 1977). They are recruited as extras to add authenticity to the prevailing account— literally in the case of "Edna the Inebriate Woman". See Shubik, 1975, p. 135: "On such occasions, and when we filmed a soup-run scene with actual men from the Hammersmith Rowton House, I began to have serious qualms about what we were doing . . . to use them and the girls from Christian Action basically as human exhibits was of dubious morality . . . I can still see Jeremy on one of his flying visits to the filming, standing wild-haired and radiant amongst the Rowton House men, lined up for a tray of BBC dinner. When several of them actually began to ask about the possibilities of a job my guilt loomed even larger".

The news media are anxious to have reliable, accredited sources to ensure the "hard facts" in which they see themselves as dealing (Glasgow University Media Group, 1976). Thus they turn to experts, which in the case of vagrancy usually means people from the correctional agencies who provide the correctional view (Elliott, 1972). In his discussion of a television production's "contact chain", Elliot shows production staff as largely reliant on chance personal contacts and organisations for information on their subject. His study also suggests that access to TV is largely restricted to those with middle-class verbal skills. Vagrants' low status extends to them as a news source. Important people, on the other hand, are eminently newsworthy, and for this reason agencies often enlist their support, although it is also often a measure of their conformity. By their nature, the mass media are an impersonal means of communication which makes it difficult to question or to challenge the interpretation they offer.* Even on TV access programmes, it has usually

---

* My thanks to Nigel Bray for this point.

been the agencies rather than their clients who have been given the floor, with the latter passing on the agency's point of view.

The whole process involved in the public presentation of vagrancy conspires to distort the phenomena included in it, and to isolate them from their structural relations. The social problem conception, itself both a cause and effect of the way the phenomena are presented, exacerbates both. By being lumped together under its heading, phenomena are divorced from their other associations. It is in the nature of a social control interpretation to isolate them in this way. They are mistakenly singled out as a separate, special class of their own. This has particularly onerous effects in the case of vagrancy where a host of heterogeneous phenomena are lumped together and consequently misconceived. Thus it is that issues of poverty, homelessness and bad housing have been isolated and lost in it.

Although it might be imagined that social policy has been essentially universalistic since the creation of the "welfare state", there has been an increasing tendency for issues to be conceived in terms of individual social problems and for social policy largely to be framed in response to them, not least because of the failure of universalistic policies and the related in-crease in a personal social services approach to problems. This has increas-ingly meant that to become a public issue, private troubles must be conceived of as social problems, rather than being avoided or dealt with in the general run of policy. The nature of the social problem conception means, however, that for something to qualify for inclusion, it must fulfil certain extraneous criteria which have more to do with that conception itself than the actual trouble involved. Judging by current social problems, it should be instantly recognisable, extraordinary, extreme, dangerous or dramatic—which means that any private trouble that does not readily match this, as few do without manipulation, is thus unlikely to become a public issue, or will be distorted out of all recognition in the process of making it one. Thus it is, for example, that the few people living in lodging houses are singled out for attention, while the many whose lives are constrained by the dreardom and meanness of rooming houses are ignored. But as we have seen, the price to be paid for such attention under the heading of a social problem, can be stigma and discrimination.

In political terms, the social problem conception seems to serve a con-sensual purpose, giving the appearance that while there may be particular problems needing attention, the structure of society is not in question. Social policy is framed in response to exceptions rather than meeting general needs with predictable effects for those involved. We might go further and say that the social problem conception and the social policy that follows from it are inherently consensual, framing phenomena in consensus terms. We have seen in the case of vagrancy how the whole process of social prob-lem presentation takes the phenomena out of context and is tied to the *status quo*. It is *status quo* interpretations of vagrancy that predominate, and as has been shown, it is in the nature of the mass media and the process of social policy formation to confirm them. Whether we conclude that existing news values and the ideology they imply arise from the mass media's own location in the social structure or that they are the accidental outcome of the way the mass media work, they have the same conservative effect, reinforcing social control accounts of the phenomena. The public are not involved except as passive spectators. As Wright-Mill (1959) said we have become "mere media markets". Everything conspires to the reinforcement of established definitions and these definitions are rooted in the *status quo*. Vagrancy, like other social problem conceptions, serves to reshape and defuse the issues included in it.

In spite of the inherent conservatism of the system, change is possible. The old channels that communicate problems like vagrancy can be used to send new messages. More use can also be made of new lines of communication like the alternative press, taking care, though, that it is not to perpetuate the old ideas in new guise. First the specialist accounts must change. The ambivalent allegiances of these involved in their production, coupled with the decline of some of the cranks who have dominated this field, make this possible. Perhaps this book is a sign that it is already happening. It is essential to stop colluding with the conventional account of vagrancy. Aware of the process at work and the direction in which it forces us, we can avoid doing so any longer, even though the temptation remains, because it seems to offer short-term gains and is easier than alternative strategies. It is this collusion that has kept the problem in existence. It is crucial to take the phenomena from under the heading of vagrancy and to make their structural connections. They must no longer be conceived in terms of vagrancy, and people lumped together as vagrants, or some other euphemism. Such a social problem conception is destructive to the phenomena and to the people included in it. Already agencies like CHAR (1976), NACRO (1976) and the Low Pay Unit have started doing this with reports like those on the low income of single homeless people, the rights of residents in hostels and similar accommodation, and the catering trade and homeless workers. More attention and priority must be given to the views and definitions of those involved in the problem. We will only know what needs doing if we know what they see as the problem. Agencies must help them to participate in the making of policy. Organisations like CHAR can play a big part in this, they can, for example, extend to them the access they have to the media. People discriminated against as vagrants must no longer be seen as having individual ills, but political grievances. Agencies should join them in fighting for their political rather than their welfare rights. The one will not come without the other.

Acknowledgements

I would like to thank the students of my media and social policy course at Lancaster University for the ideas and insights I have gained from them, especially: Nigel Bray, Pauline Beeston, John Bloxsom, Maureen O'Sullivan, Carol Evans, "Henry" Watson, John Heywood, Pat Whitehead and also Stuart McCleod. My thanks also for their help to Nick Beacock of CHAR, Christine Rouse of the *South London Press* and Hugh Hebert, Social Services Correspondent of *The Guardian*.

References

Archard, P. (1975). "The Bottle Won't Leave You." Alcoholics Recovery Project, London.

Bakewell, J. and Garnham, N. (1970). "The New Priesthood: British Television Today." Penguin, Harmondsworth.

Barthes, R. (1972). "Myth Today." Jonathan Cape, London.

Beresford, P. (1974). Much food for thought. *Soc. Work Today*, **5** (18), 568–569.

Beresford, P. (1977). Hostile reception. *New Soc.* **41** (78), 600–601.

Brandon, D. (1974). "Homeless." Sheldon Press, London.

Brown, M. (1976). "Introduction to Social Administration in Britain." Hutchinson University Library, London.

Cameron, J. (1977). "Looking at Documentary." BBC TV Series, Programme I, 26 July.

CHAR (1976). "The Low Incomes of Single Homeless People." Evidence to the Royal Commission on the Distribution of Income and Wealth, CHAR, London.

Deakin, M. and Willis, J. (1975). Yorkshire Television, Screened 22nd July.

Deakin, M. and Willis, J. (1976). "Johnny Go Home." Futura, London.

Department of Health and Social Security (1975). "Report of the Proceedings of a Meeting to Discuss Research into the Needs of Homeless Single People." DHSS, London.

Elliott, P. (1972). "The Making of a Television Series—A Case Study in the Sociology of Culture." Constable, London.

Erlam, A. and Brown, M. (1976). "Catering for Homeless Workers." CHAR and Low Pay Unit, London.

Glasgow University Media Group (1976). "Bad News", Vol. 1. Routledge and Kegan Paul, London.

Hall, S. (1973). The determination of news photographs. *In* "The Manufacture of News, Deviance, Social Problems and the Mass Media" (Cohen, S. and Young, J., eds). Constable, London.

Hall, S. (1974). "The Structured Communication of Events." Paper for Obstacles to Communication Symposium, UNESCO, Division of Philosophy, Centre for Cultural Studies, Birmingham University.

Halloran, J. D., Elliott, P. and Murdock, G. (1970). "Demonstrations and Communication." Penguin, Harmondsworth.

Hill, A. (1977). "A Cage of Shadows." Hutchinson, London.
Hoggart, R. (1976). Foreword to Glasgow University Media Group. *In* "Bad News", Vol. 1. Routledge and Kegan Paul, London.
Holloway, J. (1970). "They Can't Fit In." Bedford Square Press, London.
Keating, P. (ed.) (1976). "Into Unknown England, 1866–1913: Selections from the Social Explorers." Fontana/Collins, London.
Lovell, A. and Hillier, J. (1972). "Studies in Documentary", No. 21, Cinema One Series. Secker and Warburg, London.
Matza, D. (1969). "Becoming Deviant." Prentice-Hall, New Jersey.
Mays, J., Forder, A. and Keidan, O. (eds) (1975). "Penelope Hall's Social Services of England and Wales." Routledge and Kegan Paul, London.
Ministry of Health (1930). "Report of the Departmental Committee on the Relief of the Casual Poor", Cmnd 3640. HMSO, London.
NACRO (1976). "Rights of Residents in Hostels and Similar Accommodation." NACRO, London.
National Assistance Board (1966). "Homeless Single Persons." HMSO, London.
Orwell, G. (1964). "Down and Out in Paris and London." Penguin, Harmondsworth.
Ribton-Turner, C. J. (1887). "A History of Vagrants and Vagrancy and Beggars and Begging." Chapman and Hall, London.
St. Mungo Community Trust (1971). Newsletter, March.
Sandford, J. (1971). "Down and Out in Britain." Peter Owen, London.
Sandford, J. (1976). "Edna the Inebriate Woman. " Marion Boyars, London.
Shubik, I. (1975). "Play for Today: The Evolution of Television Drama." Davis-Poynter, London.
Stansky, P. and Abrahams, W. (1972). "The Unknown Orwell." Constable, London.
Stewart, G. and Stewart, J. (1978). Crisis every Christmas. *Comm. Care*, **214**, 22–25.
Timms, N. (1974). Battered wives: a study of social problem definition. *In* "The Year Book of Social Policy" (Jones, K., ed.). Routledge and Kegan Paul, London.
Wallich-Clifford, A. (1974). "No Fixed Abode." Macmillan, London.
Wallich-Clifford, A. (1976). "Caring on Skid Row." Veritas Publications, Dublin.
Walton-Lewsey, E. W. (1963). "Diamonds in the Dust." London Embankment Mission.
Wilkins, L. T. (1964). "Social Deviance: Social Policy, Action and Research." Tavistock, Publications, London.
Wright-Mills, C. (1959). "The Power Elite." Oxford University Press, Oxford and New York.

G

Subject Index

Index